T0062329

Choices

The Secret to Making Wise Choices

Carolyn Rabon Gault

WESTBOW
P R E S S

WestBow Press books may be ordered through booksellers or by contacting:

WestBow Press
A Division of Thomas Nelson
1663 Liberty Drive
Bloomington, IN 47403
www.westbowpress.com
1-(866) 928-1240

ISBN: 978-1-4497-0352-3 (sc)
ISBN: 978-1-4497-0353-0 (hc)
ISBN: 978-1-4497-0351-6 (e)

Library of Congress Control Number: 2010931008

Printed in the United States of America

WestBow Press rev. date:10/19/2010

Dedication

I dedicate this book to the glory of God. Without the work and guidance of the Holy Spirit, this book would not exist.

The book is also dedicated to my beloved husband, Buddy. Without his encouragement and patience, I would never have had the perseverance to complete the task of writing a book.

I would like to dedicate this book first and foremost to my immediate family. They are as listed: Kristy, Caroline, and Benjamin Walters, and Kara, Michael, Chandler and Patrick deBorde.

The dedication is also extended to include these children dear to my heart—Momo and Soto Kitahara, children of a special Japanese family we have known for years. Also to be added are the grandchildren of my prayer partner, Millie Robards. The grandchildren are: Caroline and Walker Robards, Addie and Garrett Robards, and Fulton, Bauer, and Banks Jones.

This book is a memorial to my godly parents, William Daniel Rabon and Christine Butler Rabon. They nurtured and loved me unconditionally. My parents made sure that the love of God was present in our home. They faithfully trained me in God's way.

Acknowledgments and Thanks

It would be impossible to pinpoint precisely each piece of my collection's origins. With my heart on my sleeve, as well as in my mouth, I offer a blanket "thank you" to all the expert writers, teachers, pastors, and lecturers who have influenced my thoughts and the contents of this book.

My thanks must be extended to three other important people who helped me get this book ready for publication. First, I would like to thank my precious granddaughter, Caroline Walters, for her expert help in using her computer knowledge to make this book easier to produce and submit to the publisher. Secondly, I would like to thank my good friend, Ed Knutsen, who was always ready to use his skills to keep my computer up and running. Thirdly, my dear friend, Dawna Sapp, volunteered to edit my work. She gave unselfishly of her time and used her professional knowledge to help this book be completed in the best form.

Contents

Preface

This is a book about choices. Carolyn Gault wrote *The Secret to Making Wise Choices.* Not only did she write this book to share Biblical wisdom and her lifetime collection of wisdom, but also, most importantly, to leave a legacy for her children, grandchildren, and future generations.

The Secret to Making Wise Choices is a book for our own moments of history as we face choices that are confusing in our rapidly changing culture. The future generations need as much understanding and guidance as possible in making the choices they face day by day.

The author has included choices people face during their lives. The book contains practical ways to make wiser choices. The author demonstrates how choices affect the quality of people's lives; the lives of their families, their friends, and their neighbors; and their communities. Not only does the author inform the readers how choices made in their lifetime affect their earthly lives, but also how their choices affect their place in eternity.

Introduction

Choices, choices, choices! Our whole life is consumed by choices. Each day God chooses to let us live, we will make choices in every aspect of our lives. God made us in his image. He gave us the ability to make our own choices. He did not create us to be like robots. We have the ability to choose a life which honors and glorifies Him or choose a life which is disobedient and disappointing to God. We can choose to be happy and positive or grumpy and negative. We can choose to make a life better for those we come in contact with, or we can choose to make life difficult for those around us. *The choice is ours._

Every day, we have to choose how we will deal with our circumstances—good and bad. Good circumstances in our lives make us happy. The unplanned and unwanted circumstances in our lives are the challenges. There are two ways we can deal with the challenges of bad circumstances. We can worry, fret, and be negative, or we can trust God and let him work things out for our good. The author was given a bookmarker with a quote from the well- known Christian author, Richard Exley. He rightly said, "We can hug our hurts and make a shrine out of our sorrows, or we can offer them to God as a sacrifice of praise." *The choice is ours.*

The choices we make today produce the consequences we must face tomorrow. We must make wise choices today in order not to reap bad circumstances later. Paul says in Galatians 6:7, "Whatsoever a man sows, that he will also reap." We must choose wisely, because often our choices have a reach and impact we could never imagine.

We are all human. None of us are perfect. Some of our choices will be good, and some will be bad. Our wise choices will make happier lives for ourselves and those around us. Bad choices can ruin lives. The important thing to remember is to learn from our bad choices and not repeat the same mistakes. We must choose to accept the consequences of our actions and resolve to make the future better.

We cannot underestimate the impact of our choices. Even a small choice can produce lifelong consequences for good or bad. My own mother's act of childhood disobedience to her father's orders not to climb a huge tree in their yard forever changed her ability to play the violin. Her wrist was badly broken. After the fall, she could never hold the violin properly. She had to choose the piano as her musical instrument.

Many lives can be changed forever by a choice to murder, drive drunk, use drugs, commit adultery, fornicate, lie, and steal.

The author believes the three most important of life's choices are the following:

1. The choice of the direction and focus of our lives.
2. The choice of a career.
3. The choice of a marriage partner.

A mistake in making any of these three major choices can have devastating consequences. Therefore, we need to carefully and diligently seek the wisest possible choices in these important areas in our lives.

What is the formula for making wise choices? We must read God's word. King Solomon says in Proverbs 1:7, "The fear of the Lord is the beginning of knowledge." Wisdom comes from the Lord.

God has promised in his word to give us wisdom in our choices—if we ask Him. James, one of the twelve disciples of Jesus, says in James 1:5, "If any of you lack wisdom, let him ask of God, that gives to all men generously and without reproach, and it will be given him."

Prayerfully reading and studying God's Word leads to wise choices.

The Origin of Choice

The origin of choice began at creation. "In the beginning God created the heavens and the earth" (Genesis 1:1). God is love, and his power is awesome and unlimited. God created the earth from nothing. God set the borders of the earth. The Spirit of God moved over the waters. He measured the waters in the hollow of his hand. He divided the sea by his power. God created the expanse above the earth, and he called it heaven. God alone spread out the curtains of heaven. By his Spirit, he garnished the heavens. He made Arcturus, Orion, and Pleiades, and he made the chambers of the south. He hung the stars in place, and he knows the name of each one. God stretched out the north of heaven over the empty place. God placed the sun in the heavens to give light in the day. He placed the moon in the heavens to give light at night. God created all the vegetation, plants, and trees. God created all living creatures in the sea and the birds in the air.

God created people on the sixth day. God chose to create people. People did not choose God. God chose to create people in his own image.

In the beginning, God created humans sinless and perfect. People were created lower than the angels. God created us to love and glorify Him. In addition to loving and glorifying God, people were given the responsibility to be good stewards of his creation.

God showed people the power and majesty of all creation. The beauty of God's creation can be seen in the mountain ranges, the sea, and the spectacular sunrises and sunsets. The mysteries of nature are seen in the intricate details of a spider's web, the flight patterns of geese, and the systematic beauty in the changes of the seasons. All of God's creation renders to our need to acknowledge God's awesome power by worshiping and glorifying Him.

God's original plan was for people to have a perfect relationship with Him. God gave people the responsibility to represent Him in taking care of all creation. Humans were to rule over the earth's animals, minerals, and vegetation in a manner that would bring glory to God. The earth's resources are to be used wisely. Stewardship of creation is a gift from God. We will be held responsible for his treatment of all the earth's resources.

People were created special, wonderful, and in the image of God. By God's word, humans were created by God's own personal decision within the Godhead. God formed the first man from the dust of the ground. Then God personally "breathed into his nostrils the breath of life" (Genesis 2:7). The man then became a living soul. Life is a direct gift from God.

The creation of the first man, Adam, on the sixth day, would create the fall of humankind. God knew from the beginning of creation that the perfect man he created in his image would choose to disobey Him. God knew at the time of creation that he would have to provide a way to restore people's broken, sinful relationship with God back to a personal relationship which would honor and glorify Him. The Trinity—God the Father, Jesus the Son, and the Holy Spirit—were all present at creation. God's love for people was so great, he sent his only begotten Son into the world to save sinful people. Jesus, God's Son, was willing to leave the riches of Heaven to make the perfect sacrifice for people's sins. "For God so loved the world, that he gave his only begotten Son, that whosoever believeth in Him, should not perish, but have everlasting life" (John 3:16).

God chose to create people in his own image. God created people to have a physical body, a soul, and a spirit. A person's body is their conscious life. The soul is composed of his intellect, mind, emotions, sensibility, and the power of choice or will. People are immortal and carry the special image of God in all three components. All parts of a person work in unity. Interestingly, God is three, but one in the Trinity.

Dr. Henry Morris, a great scientist, brilliant author, and a foremost advocate for Biblical creationism, writes, "There is something about the human body which is uniquely appropriate to God's manifestation of Himself, and since God knows all his works from the beginning (Acts 15:18), he must have designed man's body with this in mind."

The human body was the form in which God the Son would be incarnated or made into the likeness of men (Philippians 2:7). God knew at creation that he Himself would one day assume the form of a perfect man. God—through his Son, Jesus—would live on earth to show imperfect people how to obey God, love, and serve others. The life, death, and resurrection of Jesus would be the atonement for the sins of humankind and would restore the perfect relationship with God.

People do not have a physical likeness of God. God is a spirit (John 4:24), and God does not have a body like a human. However, when God appeared to people in the Old Testament, he appeared in the form of a man (Genesis 18:1–2; 32:24, 28, 30).

God gave people an intellectual ability superior to any animal. A person's mind is capable of communication with Him. People can pray and worship the God of creation. People can respond to God with love and devotion. God gave people a will, which enables us to choose to obey or disobey Him. God gave people the ability to govern his creation. God entrusted us to be good stewards and represent Him on earth.

A human is the only one of God's creatures who has a spirit, or God's consciousness. The spirit of a person gives them the ability to commune with God through prayer, praise, and worship. After the fall of humankind in Genesis 3, people had a moral awareness of good and evil. A person had a conscience within their spirit. Before the fall, Adam was sinless and perfect before God. Adam was placed in the paradise called the Garden of Eden. God created this garden for people to live in and enjoy his creation. Adam was to enjoy the fruit of every tree in the garden—except the tree in the middle of the garden. This tree held the knowledge of good and evil. God told Adam not to eat of the fruit of the tree of good and evil. God told Adam that if he did eat of this tree, he would surely die (Genesis 3:3).

God saw that Adam needed fellowship and a helper. God made Adam fall into a deep sleep. He took a rib from Adam and made a woman to help Adam enjoy and control all his wonderful creation. Everything God created was good. There was no sin, and Adam and Eve lived in paradise with a perfect relationship with God. God enjoyed their talks and walks together in the garden. The garden was a perfect home for Adam and his wife, who he named Eve.

One day, this perfect, sinless relationship with God ended. The serpent, Satan, came to Eve and questioned her about the fruit of the trees in the garden. The serpent said to Eve, "Yea, hath God said you shall not eat of every tree in the garden?" Eve said to the serpent, "We may eat of the fruit of the trees of the garden, but of the fruit of the tree which is in the middle of the garden, God hath said, ye shall not eat of it, neither shall ye touch it, lest ye die" (Genesis 3:1–3). The serpent, who is the father of lies, said to Eve, "You shall not surely die. You will be as gods, knowing good and evil."

Eve chose to disobey God. The serpent fooled her, and Eve ate the forbidden fruit. She shared the fruit with Adam, and he ate with her. Sin and evil now existed in the world. The relationship they had with God ended at the moment of Eve's choice to disobey God. The fall of all humankind occurred in the Garden of Eden.

As a result, God swiftly punished the serpent. He became cursed above all beasts. The serpent would always crawl on its stomach and would eat dust all its life.

The woman's punishment was sorrow in conception and in bringing forth children. The husband would rule over her.

The man's punishment was hard work. God told Adam, "Cursed is the ground for thy sake; in sorrow thou shall eat of it all the days of thy life; thorns also thistles shall it bring forth to thee; and thou shall eat the herb of the field; in the sweat of the face shall thou eat bread, till thou return to the ground; for out of it wast thou taken: for dust thou art, and into dust shalt thou return" (Genesis 3:14–19).

God's paradise for humans was destroyed by the sin of disobedience by Adam and Eve. All of Adam's descendants live in a fallen, imperfect world. Sorrow, pain, and death are permanently a part of life's journey on earth. All men and women have the problem of original sin. 1 John 1:8 says, "If we say that we have no sin, we are deceiving ourselves, and the truth is not in us."

The good news is that God gave people a second chance to live with Him in paradise! Even though people disappointed God, his love for us provided a way for our atonement of sin. John 3:16 says, "For God so loved the world, that he gave his on Begotten Son, that whosoever believeth in Him should not perish but have everlasting life."

Jesus—the Son of God—was willing to give up the riches in heaven to pay the price of people's sins. The life of Jesus on earth showed imperfect people the way to obey God, love God, and love and serve others.

The death of Jesus on the cross paid for our sins and gave forgiveness to all who choose to believe and accept Jesus as the only way to salvation.

The resurrection of Jesus from the dead after three days gave victory over the last enemy humans face—death. Jesus took the sting out of death for all who choose his gift of eternal life.

Who Am I?

Who am I? Why am I here? Where have I chosen to go when my life on earth is finished?

The first question is, "Who am I?" God created me. I am his treasured child. I was not created by accident. I was in God's thoughts and plans even before the creation of the world. I was created from the dust of the earth. God breathed into me his Spirit and gave me life. My body is the temple of the Holy God.

I have been created differently from any other person on earth. God has given me unique physical features and special gifts and talents. Just as no two fingerprints are the same, no two of God's children are created alike. I am a priceless, original masterpiece created by God.

One way I am like God's children is that I have a sinful nature. God has given me the ability to choose how I will deal with this sinful nature. I can choose to continue in my sinful, rebellious life, or I can choose to become forgiven by accepting Christ as my atonement for my sins. God hopes I will accept his plan for salvation. Peter, one of Christ's twelve disciples, says in 2 Peter 3:9, "The Lord is not slow about his promise, as some count slowness, but is patient toward you, not wishing for any to perish, but for all to come to repentance."

When I chose to accept Christ as my Savior, I had an increased worth in God's sight. I became a new self. *When I know Jesus, I know who I am!* I have been identified with Christ; I have his Holy Spirit living within me. When I read Ephesians 1:13–14, I have knowledge of my worth as a child redeemed by Christ. When I study the passage Paul wrote, I discover the following facts:

1. I have been blessed with all spiritual blessings.
2. I had been chosen before the foundation of the world.
3. I have become God's child through Christ.
4. I am accepted by Christ, just as I am.
5. I am redeemed.
6. I am forgiven.
7. I have an inheritance in heaven with Christ.
8. The Holy Spirit has sealed me.

When I know Jesus, I can say with confidence, "I am God's child, and I am loved with an everlasting love. My self-esteem comes from knowing God loves me unconditionally. I can claim the verse in Philippians 4:18, which says, 'I can do all things through Him who strengthens me.'"

The second question, "Why am I here?" is answered in the Scriptures. King Solomon, the wisest king of Israel, asked God for wisdom. God not only gave him wisdom; riches and power were also added to his life.

The longer King Solomon lived, the more he realized the futility of pleasures, possessions, and riches. King Solomon describes the futility of all the world's enticements in the book of Ecclesiastes. In these writings, he wisely wrote the truth of the purpose of humankind. In Ecclesiastes 12:18, King Solomon says, "The conclusion, when all has been heard, is: fear God and keep his commandments, because this applies to every person."

Micah, God's prophet, says in Micah 6:8 what the Lord requires of me. "But to do justice, to love kindness, and to walk humbly with my God."

In the New Testament, Jesus' life of love and service specifically show me how to accomplish my duty here on earth. Jesus says in Matthew 22:37–39, "You shall love the Lord your God with all your heart, and with all your soul, and with all your mind." Jesus says this is my first duty. The second duty is, "You shall love your neighbor as yourself."

The Sermon on the Mount is one of Jesus' most important sermons. This sermon gives a summary of my life's purpose. In the New Testament, Jesus says, "Let your light so shine before man, that they may see your good works and glorify your Father which is in heaven" (Matthew 5:16).

In conclusion, the duty of a child of God is to love and glorify God. My life is to be a witness to his grace and love. As a child of God, I show God's love when I share God's love with others.

The third question to be answered is, "Where am I going after this life ends?" When life here on earth ends, I will die. Death is a fact of life. Just as time is an equalizer, so is death. Death takes away the differences between the rich and powerful and the poor and unknown. Death levels all people. Martin Luther, the leader of the Protestant Reformation, said, "Every man must do two things alone: he must do his own believing, and his own dying."

After a person dies, earthly life is finished. Eternity begins immediately after death. In eternity, all souls return to God for judgment. The choice made on earth will determine where eternity is spent in heaven or hell.

The Bible says that heaven is a definite place God has prepared for all who have chosen to believe in Jesus Christ while on earth and have accepted his gift of forgiveness. In John 14:2–3, Jesus says, "I go to prepare a place for you. And if I go and prepare a place for you, I will come again and receive you for myself, that where I am, there you may be also."

Heaven is a place prepared for Christ's redeemed. The glory and presence of God and his love will give perfection to all things in heaven. Heaven is the Christian's eternal home. All the earth's sorrows and pain will end.

Hell is also a definite place prepared for all who refuse to accept Jesus as their Savior. Satan and all those who have chosen to live a rebellious life on earth will spend eternity in hell.

Hell is described in the Bible as a horrible punishment. John, the apostle of Christ, says in Revelation 21:8 that hell is prepared

"For the cowardly and unbelieving, and abominable, and murders, and immoral persons, and sorcerers, and idolaters, and all liars, their part will be in the lake that burns with fire and brimstone, which is the second death."

Charles H. Spurgeon, one of the greatest British preachers of his time, said, "It will be hell to a man to have his own voluntary choice confirmed, and made unchangeable."

Where you choose to spend eternity is your choice!

Life's Most Important Choice

The most important choice in life is the decision to choose the direction and focus of this life on earth. People can choose to focus their lives on the forces of good or evil.

God is the good and righteous force on earth. God loves us and created us in his own image. God has given us every good and perfect gift. God loves us unconditionally, and he has only our best interests at heart. In the Bible, the prophet Jeremiah wrote, "For I know the thoughts that I think toward you, saith the Lord, thoughts of peace, and not evil, to give you an expected end" (Jeremiah 29:11). Just think—God, our creator, thinks about us and has plans for our good. To be born in God's thought and created by Him is awesome and precious. God wants us to have a personal relationship with Him. God provided a way for our forgiveness of sin through the atonement of Jesus on the cross. When we accept the gift of salvation, God provides us eternal life with Him in heaven. Belief in Jesus gives us a life blessed in his love.

The force of all evil on earth is Satan, the adversary and enemy of God. Satan is the father of lies, the deceiver, and the man of darkness and sin. Satan's doom—and the doom of those who choose the direction of evil—was sealed when the Lord Jesus died and rose again from the dead. Satan and his followers will be cast into hell. Curses will follow them forever.

The *Charlotte Observer* features a daily column written by Billy Graham, the renowned Charlotte-born evangelist. In one of these columns, a reader wrote to Mr. Graham and asked him if the devil is real. He gave the following explanation: "There is much about the devil we don't fully understand." However, "the Bible makes it clear that the he is absolutely evil, and ultimately he is behind all the evil that goes on in the world." The Bible reveals that God is "the spirit who is now at work in those who are disobedient to God" (Ephesians 2:2).

Mr. Graham gives three truths about the devil. "First, Satan is real. He isn't a vague, impersonal force; he is a powerful spiritual being with a real personality—which means he can scheme and plot against us. Second, the devil has one main goal: to oppose God and his will for our lives. Sometimes Satan's temptations seem very attractive, but in the end they will lead us away from God. The Bible calls Satan 'that ancient serpent—who leads the whole world astray' (Revelation 12:9). Never forget; the devil is not your friend, but your foe. But the Bible tells us the final truth about the devil; he is a defeated foe! By his death and resurrection, Jesus conquered Satan and broke his hold over us."

The most important choice we make in life is to accept God's gift of love to redeem us from our sins. God's love, as written in the Bible, includes the help we need to gain wisdom in making this most important choice. God left us the Bible. The Bible is God's voice speaking to our heart through the Holy Spirit. The Holy Spirit convicts us of the fact that we are sinners and need God's forgiveness.

The Apostle Paul was known as the Apostle to the Gentiles. He was one of the world's greatest preachers, and he helped organize the first Christian churches. His missionary journeys spread Christianity throughout all the surrounding regions. Many of Paul's letters form a large part of the New Testament. Paul says it is the Gospel that transforms us into the renewed image of God. We cannot become transformed in righteousness and holiness by our own efforts, but through receiving Christ in faith and repentance. John, one of the twelve disciples of Jesus, says in John 1:12, "But as many as received Him, to them gave the power to become the sons of God, even to them that believe on his name." Paul writes in Ephesians 2:8, "For by grace ye are saved through faith; and that not of yourselves; it is the gift of God." Titus 3:5 says, "Not by works of righteousness which we have done, but according to his mercy he saved us, by the washing of regeneration, and the renewing of the Holy Spirit." The work of the Holy Spirit speaks to our heart and leads us to make the choice to accept Christ as our Savior. The moment we choose Christ, the Holy Spirit (God Himself) resides in our heart. Accepting Christ changes our lives and our destiny. Our lives are forever sealed by his love and forgiveness. The Holy Spirit within a believer gives them wisdom to make right choices. The next chapter will tell us about the Holy Spirit.

The Holy Spirit

The Holy Spirit is God Himself living in the life of the believer. The Holy Spirit is the third person in the Trinity. He is just as much God as God the Father and God the Son. The Holy Spirit applies the salvation that was provided by God the Father through the death on the cross of Jesus, his for our forgiveness of sins. The work of the Holy Spirit sets sinners apart from sin and remakes them for God's service. Matthew Henry said, "All the Holy Spirit's influences are heaven begun, glory in seed and bud." Maurice A. P. Wood said, "The Holy Spirit loves so to arrange men's circumstances that they are brought within the sphere of God's influence."

God wants all of his followers to live a life that glorifies Him. In addition to forgiveness, God gives us the Holy Spirit's power in our lives to help us live victoriously. The Holy Spirit is sometimes referred to as the helper (John 16:5–7). Jesus promised his followers that after his death and resurrection, he would send the helper. In Acts 2, on the day of Pentecost, the gift of the Holy Spirit was given to all the believers. "Before Pentecost, the disciples found it hard to do easy things, after Pentecost, they found it easy to do hard things." This quote by A. J. Gordon shows the importance of the Holy Spirit's presence in the believer's heart.

After Pentecost, Peter was filled with the Holy Spirit's presence. He preached the powerful sermon: "Repent, and let each of you be baptized in the name of Jesus Christ for the forgiveness of your sins, and you shall receive the gift of The Holy Spirit."

The hearts of the disciples were changed when the Holy Spirit came into their lives, and they received the power of God Himself to do his work on earth.

The good news is that the Holy Spirit is present in every true believer's heart today. Lionel Fletcher, in the book *Gathered Gold,* gave this quotation, "The Christian's birthright is the power of the Holy Ghost." Every believer has the power of God in them to face all the crisis of our lives here on earth. The Holy Spirit is the source of the believer's help in fighting the old, sinful nature. Even though the sinner is "born again," he or she still has some of their old self-living within. The old and new self will be in constant conflict. The conflict within is called spiritual warfare. The duty of the Holy Spirit in a believer's life is to guide the believers to obey and honor God with their choices. God knew the believers could not possibly obey Him without the help of his Holy Spirit. "It is God who is all the while effectually at work in you, energizing and creating in you the power and desire—both to will and to work for his good and pleasure and satisfaction and delight." (*The Amplified Bible*, Philippians 2:12-13) Without the Holy Spirit within us, we can do no good thing. John Wesley was the leader of the evangelical revival and founder of the Methodist church in Great Britain and America. He said, "Without the Spirit of God we can do nothing but add sin to sin."

In order for the Holy Spirit to work in a believer's life more effectively, the believer needs to develop a daily intimate prayer life and the practice of daily Bible reading. When the believer searches the Scriptures, the Holy Spirit's attention and guidance is given to the believer. The Bible's wisdom helps the believer make wise choices and keeps them from the destructive ways of sin. John Bunyun, an English preacher, who wrote the religious allegory *The Pilgrim's Progress* rightly said, "The Bible keeps one from sin, and sin keeps one away from the Bible."

Chosen holy people, directed by the Holy Spirit Himself, wrote the Bible. The Holy Spirit guides lives with the wisdom and authority of the Scriptures. His guidance never conflicts with the truths of the Bible. 2 Timothy 3:16 says, "All scripture is given by the inspiration of God, and is profitable for doctrine, for reproof, for correction, for instruction in righteousness."

There will be times a believer will not know how to make a right choice. When the believer goes to God's word, James, a disciple of Christ, writes, "If any of you lack wisdom, let him ask of God, who gives to all men generously and without reproach, and it will be given him" (James 1:5). The reading of Scripture will give guidance and wisdom from The Holy Spirit. R. Tinlayson, in the book *Gathered Gold,* says, "The Spirit gives personal guiding, especially in and by reason and conscience in the Word, and as a guide, he is sufficient. He is an eternal guide. He throws all the light that we need upon the character of desires and actions, upon the path of duty." If a person has the Holy Spirit in their heart and the Bible in their hand, they can make wiser choices.

The Choice of a Marriage Partner

The choice of a marriage partner is the second most important decision made in a person's life.

In the mobile world we live in today, it is rare that a woman marries a man from her hometown. The complexities of social, religious, and economic differences are apparent in all societies of our world today. Transportation and new technological ways of communication have made our world global. In just a few hours, anyone can fly to any destination in the civilized world. E-mail is sent across the world to another computer or cell phone in a matter of seconds. Some young people are even using computer sites to find prospective mates for themselves! Text messages on cell phones are another way to send someone an instant message.

American cities and towns have changed to reflect this global influence upon our social, religious, and economic ideas. As a result, young people today are faced with many ideas strangely different than their parents' earlier thoughts on the world around them.

Our country was founded on Christian principles. The values and morals of Christian ethics were ingrained in society.

Today, these principles are being questioned and even silenced in our schools and colleges. What a challenge it is today to stand up for Christian beliefs. The words "tolerance" and "politically correct" have become the world's standards.

Many non-Christians living in America have had an impact on our young people's lives. There are now more foreign students in our high schools and colleges. These students have cultures that are drastically different from our Christian values.

Young adults entering college are especially vulnerable to different ideas from culturally diverse fellow students. These college students are placed in classes together, and they interact in social events together. They become friends, and some eventually marry. The cultural, social, and religious differences are a real challenge to their marriages. A marriage can only survive if each person truly seeks the other's happiness over their own and is willing to compromise.

When a person looks for a marriage partner, they should try to eliminate challenging differences. Marriage can be difficult even when a perspective mate has the same family profile. Look for the same morals and religious beliefs.

Christians, Jews, and Muslims are all followers of the God of Abraham. The major difference between these three faiths is the life of Jesus Christ. Jews and Muslims believe he was a holy man, and some say he was a prophet. Jesus Christ, to a Christian, is the holy Son of God. Christians believe Jesus' life, death, and resurrection are their only hope in this world and the world to come. Christians believe that Jesus Christ is the only means of salvation. 1 John 4:15 says, "Whosoever shall confess that Jesus is the Son of God, God dwelleth in him, and he in God." Romans 10:9 says, "That if thou shalt confess with thy mouth the Lord Jesus, and believe in thine heart that God hath raised Him from the dead, thou shalt be saved."

Christians must realize that some of these prospective mates can have wonderful qualities. They can be physically attractive, intelligent, protective, and romantic. In fact, they can have all the qualities desired in a mate—except their belief in God's Son, Jesus, as the only way to salvation.

Christians are warned in the Bible to marry only believers. In 1 Corinthians 6:14) the words say, "Be ye not unequally yoked together with unbelievers." Do not be fooled—a Christian cannot marry an unbeliever and please God.

There are four important requirements Christians should consider in choosing a marriage partner.

1. The marriage partner must be a like-minded, God-fearing, Spirit-filled Christian.
2. The marriage partner should come from a family of integrity.
3. Choose a marriage partner who is ready to assume the demands and added responsibilities marriage requires.
4. Choose a marriage partner who is capable of giving love unconditionally.

The first requirement for a marriage partner is that they must be a like-minded, God-fearing, Spirit-filled Christian. There can be no compromise on this important element in a marriage.

A word of caution—not all Christians are like-minded. Some Christians should not marry other Christians, if there are some differences they cannot comprise on.

Protestants and Catholics are both Christians. However, the views of each of these churches are very different. Intermarriage can be successful if the couple is willing to undergo counseling together. They must seek to come to a mutual agreement in which both of them will be happy. The counseling should be done before the engagement is announced. The agreement should be made before the marriage. Children born into a marriage deserve to have parents united in their faith.

There are differences in the Protestant faith. Baptists, Methodists, Presbyterians, Lutherans, and Episcopalians have different views. If the couple is not of the same Protestant faith, they need to decide on which of their churches they will attend together. They can even mutually agree to visit several churches together. After visiting the churches, they can choose which church they both feel meets their spiritual needs. If the couple cannot agree to be unified in their faith, it is time to reevaluate their commitment to becoming united in marriage. If unity in worship is very important to their happiness, it is time to consider breaking up and dating others.

What are the two non-compromises for a couple who are professing Christians? First, both must believe that Jesus Christ is the only way to salvation. Salvation is by grace through faith in Jesus Christ. Nothing is added as a requirement for salvation. Paul, the apostle, states in Ephesians 2:8–9, "For by grace are ye, saved through faith; and that not of yourselves: it is the gift of God. Not have works, lest any man should boast." The second non-compromise is that the Scripture must be believed to be the Word of God. The original text of the Bible cannot be added to or taken from. All the events are true. They are not fables or allegories. 1 Timothy 3:16 says, "All Scripture is given by the inspiration of God, and is profitable for doctrine, for reproof, for correction, for instruction in righteousness."

The couple should agree on these two basic Christian doctrines. If the couple cannot agree on these two major issues, they are not like-minded. They need to look for someone who shares their beliefs. A church based on the beliefs of both couples is essential for a successful spiritual union in marriage.

In addition to being like-minded in their beliefs, a marriage partner needs to be Spirit-filled. Every true believer receives the Holy Spirit into their lives when they trust Jesus as their Savior. The Holy Spirit (God within the heart) is evident in the way a person acts towards others.

Paul writes in Galatians 5:22, "But the fruit of the Spirit is love, joy, peace, long suffering, gentleness, goodness, and faith, meekness, and temperance." These qualities are evident in those who are seeking to live a Christ-centered life. When these qualities are present, the marriage has a greater chance of success.

The second important element in choosing a marriage partner is to choose a family of integrity. Honesty, fairness, hard work, and kindness must be standard behavior.

Family background is extremely important. Keep in mind that the in-laws will be the grandparents of your children. They will influence your children's attitudes and behavior. Another idea to keep in mind is that most families spend holidays, birthdays, religious services, and some vacations together.

Before an engagement is announced, the couple needs to spend time with both families. Visits should be made to both homes. Weekends spent with prospective in-laws can reveal much about their home life. It is important to gain insight into how well they relate to themselves and others. Children will carry over into their marriage the same attitudes and relationships they learned from their parents.

What are some of the characteristics to look for in a family's relationships?

1. Is it apparent the father and mother are practicing Christians? Do they read the Bible as a family? Do they attend church regularly? Do they give to their church and support the church's needs? Do prayers of thanksgiving bless the meals?
2. Is it apparent there is love between the mother and the father?
3. How do the brothers and sisters treat each other? Are they kind and loyal to one another?
4. How does the family relate to their friends and neighbors? Are they friendly and hospitable, or are they reclusive?
5. What are the ideas about serving and helping those in need within their communities?

The final analyses of the family should bring positive feelings about the time spent in their company.

The third important element in choosing a marriage partner is to choose someone who will be responsible for the additional demands required to make a marriage successful. Marriage is not an emotion, but a commitment of responsibility to make sure the best interest of the other is paramount.

What are the responsibilities of the husband? The husband is to be the head of the home. The husband will be accountable to God for his wife and any children. A man should not marry until he can provide for the spiritual, emotional, and financial needs of a wife and future children.

Husbands are to love their wives as Christ loves the church. Paul writes in Ephesians 5:25, "Husbands, love your wives, even as Christ also loved the church, and gave Himself for it." Ephesians 5:28 says, "So ought men to love their wives as their own bodies. He that loveth his wife loveth himself."

What are the responsibilities of a wife to her husband? The wife is to be the helpmate to her husband. She is to love, honor, and cherish him. The husband is to rule over his wife with love, and she is to submit to his God-given authority. He must remember to respect her needs and love her. The husband should desire the wife's happiness above his own.

The wife is who is loved and protected by her husband is to respond by helping him establish a loving atmosphere. Her desire as a wife is to make her husband's happiness more important than her own.

The wife is responsible for keeping an orderly home. Usually, the wife prepares the meals and makes sure the clothing is ready for wearing. The wife provides for the care of the children.

A mother's influence on the children is extremely important. She sets the tone and atmosphere of the home. A home with a mother who nurtures and loves her children will be rewarded with happy and confident adults. The mother is to reinforce the father's godly leadership.

The fourth important requirement in choosing a marriage partner is to choose a person capable of loving unconditionally. Lasting, true love is unconditional. There are two kinds of love—conditional and unconditional.

In *The Presbyterian Journal,* September 8, 1982, there was an article called "Love, Marriage, and Divorce"_which discussed conditional and unconditional love. *The Presbyterian Journal* gave an excellent description of the difference between the two types of love. The author saved this article for her own children and grandchildren to read.

The following is the way *The Journal* describes the two kinds of love: "Conditional love is like an exchange. For example, 'I love you'—*if* you meet my needs, *if* you are nice to me, or *if* you respect me. This type of conditional love depends on how you treat one another." Another way to describe conditional love is: "I love you *because* you are handsome, beautiful, intelligent, successful, famous, and you give me nice gifts." Of course, this type of conditional "love" doesn't create a lasting relationship. What happens when competition and comparison to others makes someone else more appealing? A third way to describe conditional love is, "I love you *as soon as* you meet my expectations." You must measure up to certain manners, a social position, or a level of education. None of the above named conditions—*if, because,* or *as soon as*—have anything to do with real love. They are counterfeits!

Real love is without conditions. You are loved just the way you are, in spite of who you are, or for no particular reason.

How does one become capable of giving unconditional love? Only a person who has experienced God's unconditional love and grace can love themselves and become capable of giving unconditional love to a marriage partner. God's unconditional love in gives security, peace, and love in a person's heart.

Make sure the prospective marriage partner has experienced the unconditional love and peace that a commitment to Christ brings to their life. Only then can they love unconditionally—and for the right reason.

The Institution of Marriage

The institution of marriage began with God. God performed the first marriage ceremony. God created the first man, Adam, and placed him in the Garden of Eden. Even though the Garden of Eden was a perfect paradise, Adam was very lonely. He needed someone to be his helpmate. Adam needed another person with a soul like his to love and share the beautiful home God had prepared for him.

God saw Adam's need for love and companionship. God decided to create a helpmate for Adam. While Adam was in a deep sleep, God removed a rib from Adam and created Eve from his body. Eve was called woman because she was taken from Adam's body.

God's creation now included a man and a woman. God created them male and female. The male's physical body was designed so he could be the aggressor or initiator. The female's body was designed so she could be the receiver of the man's initiation. The physical differences between the male and female were designed to compliment each other in marriage.

In Elizabeth Elliot's book, *Passion and Purity,* she writes, "Adam and Eve made a mess of things when the reversed roles. She took the initiative, offered him the forbidden fruit, and he—instead of standing as her protector—responded and sinned along with her." The rest is history; there has been confusion and turmoil ever since.

The institution of marriage was an important time to celebrate in the time of Jesus. After the vows were taken, the guests stayed two to three days to talk, eat, and drink.

Mary, the mother of Jesus, and Jesus and his friends were invited to a wedding in the little village of Cana. Many other people were also. In fact, more people came than were expected. Before the feast was over, the servants realized they did not have enough wine for all the guests. They were troubled.

Mary heard about the embarrassing problem. She knew Jesus could help if he chose to use the great power she believed Him to possess.

Mary did not ask Jesus to help. She just told Jesus simply, "They have no wine." Mary asked the servants to obey whatever Jesus asked them to do. She felt confident Jesus would help save the family the embarrassment of not being prepared to serve all their guests.

There were six stone jars filled with household water. Jesus told the servants to fill the jars with fresh water. He then told them to take a taste of the contents from the jars to the ruler of the feast.

The servants obeyed Jesus. They were astonished when the miracle of wine was poured from the jars. The servants quickly carried the new wine to the ruler of the feast. When the ruler of the feast tasted the wine the servants obtained from the water jars, he called the young man giving the wedding feast. He asked the young man why "the best wine was saved until last." Normally the best wine was served first.

Jesus' first miracle was performed quietly at a wedding ceremony. Only Jesus' mother and the amazed servants could have known a miracle had occurred.

Choose Real Love

God is love. God is not faith or hope; God is love.

We cannot know real love unless we go to the source. You cannot get light from a lamp unless it is plugged into the socket. The only way you can know God's love is to commit your life to Him day by day and put our confidence in Him rather than in other people.

Paul, in Galatians 5:22, lists love as the first fruit of The Spirit, and from this root will grow all the other attributes listed in Galatians. God is love. Real love must start with God.

Oswald Chambers, a Scottish minister, teacher, and author, says, "The springs of love are in God, not in us. It is absurd to look for the love of God in our hearts naturally; it is only there when it has been shed abroad in our hearts by the Holy Spirit."

What are the characteristics of real love? The Bible gives us the definition of godly love in 1 Corinthians 13:4–7. "Love is patient and kind. Love is not jealous or boastful or proud or rude. Love does not demand its own way. Love is not irritable, and it keeps no record of when it has been wronged. It is never glad about injustice but rejoices whenever the truth wins out. Love never gives up, never loses faith, it is always hopeful, and endures through every circumstance."

When we read this chapter, we do not see a worldly concept of "warm fuzzes." We see love not as a feeling or an emotion, but we see love as a commitment with responsibilities to provide the best interest of the other person over self-interest. The spiritual love shown in this passage is from God Himself and is given to us as an example for our daily lives.

What God's Word says about the responsibilities of true love can be found in Romans 12:9–12. These Bible verses can be a guide to help a person love in a godly manner. "Let love be without hypocrisy. Abhor what is evil; cling to what is good. Be devoted to one another in brotherly love; give preference to one another in honor; not lagging behind in diligence, fervent in spirit, serving the Lord; rejoicing in hope, persevering in tribulation, devoted to prayer."

True love is genuine respect of another. True love is devotion to another's needs before your own. True love perseveres in times of trials.

We need to use the word *love* in the correct way. Today some people use the word in shallow ways. They say, "I love my car," "I love my house," "I love chocolate," or "I love a funny story." You only have to look on the car bumper stickers to see a red heart which is followed by a declaration of love for a sport, school, college, dog, or anything else the car owner loves.

In earlier years, the word *like* was used to describe worldly things. The word *love* was used specifically for a person who was very close or dear.

What conclusions can we give about deep, true love? God is love. God so loved the world that he sent his only Son, Jesus, into the world to show us how to love Him and each other. Only when we put our hope in Jesus and maintain the habit of prayer and reading his Word daily can we give or receive love in the manner Jesus gives love to us. Daily prayer and Bible reading allow the Holy Spirit to fill our hearts with his love, his life, and his power. Only by abiding in his love can we begin to experience the wonderful blessing of knowing Jesus and what it is like to love another person God's way.

Ask some serious questions before saying, "I love you." Is your love patient and kind? Can your love stand the trials of adversity and still love? Can your love withstand discouragement and failure on the part of others? Does your love follow God's plan for fulfilling the responsibilities required to have a successful marriage? If your relationship with Jesus includes studying his Word and a true commitment to serve Him, your love for Jesus is true. A sincere love and desire to serve Jesus gives a person the ability to love a future mate.

Choices of Godly Parenting

Parents have a choice to train their children in a Godly manner or to neglect to teach them about God and his love for them. Donald Grey Barnhouse, a Presbyterian minister and widely acclaimed pioneer of radio preaching in the 1920s, rightly said, "For parents to see a child grow up without Christ is a greater dereliction of duty than for parents to have children who grow up without learning to read or write."

No man or woman has ever had a nobler challenge or higher privilege than to bring up a child for God. Every child's life starts out with a strong pull either for good or evil. A child's attitudes about God, themselves, and the world around them are greatly influenced by their parents. How children see things depends on what their parents teach them.

The Bible says that "children are a gift from God." The child who is trained and molded into God's image is the parent's gift back to God. No parent should take lightly their God-given authority to love and discipline their children.

The book *Shepherding a Child's Heart* by Tedd Tripp is an excellent book on guiding a child's heart and molding them into the image of God. Tripp talks about the child-parent relationship. The parent is given authority by God to act as his agent on earth to shepherd their child's heart to understand God's unconditional love for them and the grace of the Gospel.

The authority given to parents requires them to shepherd the child's heart to be obedient to God and the parents' authority. In

Ephesians 6:1–2, the Bible says, "Children, obey your parents in the Lord, for this is right. Honor thy Father and Mother." Proverbs 13:24 states, "He that spares the rod hates his son, but he that loves him chasteneth him betimes." Proverbs 22:6 says, "Train up a child in the way he should go; and when he is old, he will not depart from it."

Parents who choose to raise godly children must look at the ways they can supply their children's needs. John Maxwell, an expert speaker and author who has sold over thirteen million books, wrote in the March 1998 *Decision Magazine* an article about the six things children need. The six needs given to help raise obedient, godly children are:

1. Constructive discipline
2. Unconditional love
3. Quality time spent as a family
4. Role models with godly traits
5. Attention and respect
6. Prayer

The first need, constructive discipline, is very important in order to have obedient children. When parents love their children, they give constructive discipline. The children respond by giving their parents respect and obedience. Love equals discipline. Discipline done with love is constructive and is never done in anger. Parents should cool down before confronting their child. The Bible says, "Provoke not your child to anger." (Colossians 3:21) When parents scream, beat their children, and say things like, "I've had it with you," "You never do anything right," or "You're a loser," this is negative discipline. Negative discipline never corrects the behavior.

What is constructive discipline? Constructive discipline corrects the wrong behavior without punishing the child in anger. When parents discipline with love, it corrects the bad behavior and results in respect and love for the child's parents. Godly discipline with love results in their children feeling secure and self-confident.

Parents must be unified in their discipline. The children must understand that their parents will stand firmly together. There should be no thought of one parent's "yes" and the other parent's "no!" Lack of unity between parents will cause children to be insecure and confused.

Parents need to be concerned not only with the behavior of their children but also with the attitude of their hearts. The attitude of a child's heart is very important. Your child's heart makes him or her a unique person. The heart controls his or her affection, conscience, thought processes, motives, and actions. Your child's conscience gives them their sense of right and wrong.

Parents need to tell the child what they did wrong. The child should understand that their disobedience was to Gods authority figure, the parent. The parent needs to show the child that not obeying their parents is also being disobedient to God.

The parents need to explain why the child's actions were disobedient. They were disobedient because all God's children have a sinful nature at birth. Parents need to guide their children to see the need to confess their sins to God and ask Him for forgiveness. Children need to know that confession of sin to Jesus will give them forgiveness and a new, clean heart.

The story was told about a little boy who had just been tucked into bed by his mother, who was waiting to hear his prayers. The little boy had been very naughty that day, and his conscience was bothering him. He said, "Mama, I wish you'd go now and leave me alone. I want to pray by myself." The mother could tell something was wrong. She asked her son if there was something he needed to tell her. The son said, "No, Mommy. You would just scold me, but God will forgive me and forget about it." The little boy understood the love, grace, and forgiveness as shown in the Gospel.

God's discipline is for correction and instruction. Discipline by God can be painful, but the results can be an amazing transformation of the heart. Parents must discipline with the same goals as God. Constructive discipline given by parents is not to be administered as a punishment, but for correction and instruction.

Parents must choose to meet their child's second need for unconditional love. Homes, which provide unconditional love, create children who feel secure and significant. The unconditional love of parents must be modeled by God's love for them. Parents should love their children simply because they are a gift from God and their own flesh and blood. They are not to be loved according to their behavior, potential, or performance.

God's love for us is unconditional. He loves us in spite of our sinful selves. God loves us when we are obedient and when we fall short of his hopes for us. God keeps on loving us, because he knows we need his love—especially when we do not deserve it!

The best example of unconditional parental love in the Bible is the story of the Prodigal Son. The father never gave up on his wayward son; he didn't judge his bad behavior. He welcomed him home with unconditional, forgiving love.

Children who are given unconditional love have the advantage to grow up physically, emotionally, and psychologically secure. Children who feel secure will feel comfortable sharing important matters with their parents. They will share their hopes and dreams. They will share their fears and failures. They know their parents will love them—no matter what! Children who have experienced their parents' unconditional love feel significant, because their parents have made the children realize they are God's unique, special masterpieces.

In the May 1996 issue of *Focus on the Family,* there was an article adapted from *Faith Training* by Joe White which gave twenty ways to tell your child "I love you."

1. Snuggle in bed together as you tell a good night story.
2. The next time you take a child to an athletic practice, stay and watch from a distance.
3. Have a family worship time after a meal by singing, praying, and reading scripture together.
4. Write a crazy poem by taking turns writing the next line (make sure it rhymes).

5. At the beach or in a park sandbox, play tic-tac-toe in the sand.
6. Plant trees in your yard in honor of your kids (one for each child).
7. On a hot day, hook up a water hose and sprinkler in the backyard and run through the water together.
8. Roast marshmallows over the barbecue.
9. Show your child where you've kept a special card or picture he or she has given you for a long time.
10. Honor your child with a "just because" party ("just because I love you") and invite his or her friends.
11. Make a photo gallery somewhere in your home, and display your children's school pictures from each year.
12. Play hide-and-seek with your children (don't find them too quickly).
13. Talk with your child about what you're learning personally about Jesus Christ.
14. Take advantage of the long days and go on an evening walk together.
15. Have lunch together in the school cafeteria before the school year ends.
16. When your child talks to you, put down what you're doing and look into his or her eyes. Maintain an encouraging expression, and make your response positive.
17. At your next opportunity, give your child a hug. If your child is young, pick them up and hold them.
18. When your child says, "Watch me!"—Watch. Clap and cheer, and say, "Great job!"
19. Make a special effort to get a good view of your city's Fourth of July fireworks display.
20. Start praying now for the spouses your children will have someday. Pray that their marriages will be strong and Christ-centered.

Parents must choose to emphasize the third need of quality time with their children. Many parents give children everything except themselves.

In today's modern technological, scientific, sports-minded, and consumer-orientated world, parents face real challenges trying to compete with the many choices and attractions surrounding their families. Parents must offer children their presence rather than presents. Jennifer Coburn, a novelist, wrote about this very subject in a newspaper article. The article showed how too many toys teach children they deserve to have all "this stuff," and they become ungrateful and absorbed with themselves. Children will not remember all the presents when they are grown. They will remember the special times together as a family. Parents who can afford to spoil their children by giving too many toys are really depriving them of more creative experiences.

The technological toys can isolate children from their parent's time and attention. Many overscheduled parents allow the TV, X-Box, Wii, iPod, and cell phone to entertain their children, because they are too busy or tired to take time to talk to their children.

In the book *Born to Buy*, Juliet Schor explains how commercial culture has impacted the behavior of children. It has been noted that children with more "stuff" are more likely to suffer from depression, anxiety, headaches, stomachaches, and boredom. As these children become adolescents, their values are more likely to be materialistic.

Children with materialistic values are more likely to engage in smoking, drinking, illegal drugs, and sex. The other negatives associated with materialism can be a narcissistic attitude, separation anxiety, paranoia, and attention deficit disorder. Children with these problems do not perform as well in school, jobs, and extracurricular activities.

Parents who choose to spend more quality time with their children will limit their children's isolating toys. Parents who choose to spend quality time with their children will challenge the world's consumerism by being in control of their home atmosphere.

One way parents can control their home atmosphere is to have control over mealtime. At meals, parents and children should talk about their day's activities. They should listen to each other and genuinely care about each other's activities, concerns, and achievements.

Mealtimes are extremely important family times. Parents need to keep mealtimes free from interruptions. They need to set rules that no TV, hand-held games, or telephone calls will be tolerated at the table. The best way to handle the TV is to keep the TV out of viewing distance. The telephone calls can be put on hold until after the meal and conversations are finished. The conversations about the family's day and their concerns for each other are more important. Parents should even discuss current events at meals. William Temple, a priest of the English church, said, "The most influential of all education factors is the conversation in the home." In addition to conversations, meals are a great time to have a short devotion and prayers.

In addition to the home atmosphere, parents can choose to use "car time" to have conversations with their children. Parents can use the time on the way to and from school and time going to various after-school activities. Of course, the parents will have to silence iPods, cell phones, games, and TVs in the car.

Another important way to spend quality time as a family is to take vacations the whole family can enjoy. Swimming, golfing, boating, hiking, bicycle riding, camping, and horseback riding are just a few fun ways for families to enjoy time together. As the children grow older, traveling to national parks and historical places can be additional times to enjoy as a family.

Creating special family traditions is another way to spend quality time as a family. Parents need to continue to use traditions handed down over the years. New traditions can give families memories that will become times to enjoy and treasure.

Christmas traditions can include a family trip to the Christmas tree farm to choose just the right tree. Special time can be set aside so everyone can help decorate the tree. This is the perfect time to talk about the memories of each ornament used over the years.

After the decoration of the tree, there could be a time to share cookies and hot chocolate. The cookies could be made from old family recipes. Children love to help bake cookies. Their cookies could be used to decorate the tree.

Musical families often can share the beautiful Christmas hymns and carols around the piano. Parents can let the smallest children help ring bells to add their special touch to songs like "Jingle Bells."

In order to celebrate the real meaning of Christmas, Christian parents can buy or make an Advent wreath. One wreath can be made and used over the years. Only the candles will have to be replaced yearly. During the weeks of Advent, let each family member take turns reading the Scriptures which apply to the truths of Christ's birth. The lighting of the candles is a way to teach children that Jesus is "the light of the world."

Parents need to teach their children early the real meaning of Christmas. It is not all about them and the gifts they receive. They need to know that Christmas is about love. Jesus came into the world to show us how to love Him and share his love with others.

The parents should make it a tradition to teach children to locate the needy in the church and community. The children could be asked to assist their parents in distribution of food and clothing to those less fortunate. Children can help fill shoeboxes sent by Samaritan's Purse. These boxes are sent all over the world at Christmas time. The children who receive these boxes feel the love of Jesus, and also receive gifts of their very own.

Parents can have the tradition of sharing a meal at Christmas with the lonely and elderly. In college towns, there are many foreign students who attend international church dinners. Church members can "adopt" them for holiday meals with their families.

Easter is another Christian tradition to be shared with the family. Little children can learn about the new life in Christ by hunting plastic Easter eggs, which have hidden in them the special items relating to Christ's death and resurrection. These eggs can be bought in Christian bookstores or in some churches. Children love to hunt the eggs, and at the same time, they gain the true meaning of Easter.

Traditions celebrating a family member's birthday are very special to the family. Favorite cakes and foods can be made over the years. Surprise trips and parties can be fun.

Parents can make sporting events become a traditional part of their family's fun time together. "Tailgate food" shared with family and friends make a good social time.

National holidays like the Fourth of July, Memorial Day, Labor Day, Mother's Day, and Father's Day are some of the special times families can enjoy spending together. Children should be taught the real meaning of these special days.

Parents who choose to spend quality time with their children will earn a lifetime of respect and love. After the children are grown and married, they will still want to come for visits and fun together. The memories of family fun and togetherness will last a lifetime and spill over to the next generations.

The fourth need of children is the need of a Christian role model in their parents. Albert Schweitzer, a famous theologian, philosopher, and physician, said, "Example is not the main thing in influencing others; it is the only thing."

Parents who display a love and obedience for God will encourage their children to exhibit the same behaviors. Parents who model the characteristics of truthfulness, love, and kindness will raise children who will use their parents' lives as a copybook.

Parents who wisely put a high price on truthfulness in their own relationships will encourage their children to hold high the standards of truthfulness in their own lives. Parents must be careful to avoid false excuses in work or social events. In the home, children should never hear one parent lie about the other parent. Children quickly learn to embroider false stories by listening to bad parenting choices about the truth. Parents must be completely truthful in all their behavior. Phillip Brooks said, "Truth is always strong, no matter how weak it looks, and falsehood is always weak, no matter how strong it looks." Truth is always the strongest argument.

Children must be taught to never lie, even if telling the truth causes them to suffer harsh consequences. Truth must always be presented as the strongest argument. It was once said, "When you tell the truth, you will never have to remember what you said."

The Bible has harsh words for a lying tongue. King Solomon wrote in Proverbs 12:19, "The lip of truth shall be established forever:

but a lying tongue is but for a moment." He also says in Proverbs 12:22, "Lying lips are abomination to the Lord: but they that deal truly are his delight."

In addition to truthfulness, parents are a child's earliest remembrances of love and kindness. Very young children learn kindness and compassion by simply watching and experiencing their parents' kindness and love for them.

Parents cannot control when someone does something kind for them. However, they can control when they show kindness to someone else. Children soon learn the same principle about kindness. They learn quickly that kindness makes their lives much happier. It has been said, "Kindness is the oil that takes the friction out of life."

What are some of the ways parents can teach positive ways of kindness and compassion for others? One way a parent can let a child experience kindness is to include them when you visit a retirement or nursing home. The residents will love your child. A smiling, curious child will bring joy to their hearts. Older children can be encouraged to help stir the batter for the goodies carried to share. Let the children pass out the treats.

Teenagers can help volunteer at the food bank. Let them help fill the bags of groceries and give out the filled bags. Teens love to shop. Let them help shop for clothes for the needy. They will know how to pick clothing other children will enjoy wearing.

Another way parents set an example of kindness is by being good neighbors. When the neighbors are away, the parents can feed pets, water flowers, and get the neighbors' mail and newspapers. When a neighbor is sick or elderly, sharing a meal with them often is just the encouragement they need. It has been said, "If Christ is in your home, the neighbors will know."

Parents who are friendly are showing kindness to those they meet. Parents who welcome newcomers to their neighborhoods and churches are good role models for their children. When the children grow older, a new child at school, a new teammate, or a new child at church will benefit because of their parents' example.

Parents who take the opportunity to share their home with visiting missionaries give their children exposure to God's special ministers of the Gospel. Missionaries are wonderful models for the children's spiritual growth. Missionaries also teach your children about other countries around the world.

Parents who teach their children kindness and compassion will raise children who are givers rather than takers.

Children leave home after only a few years. Parents must realize they are raising their children to live with someone else! Parents who raise loving and kind children send them out into the world with the ability to have a successful marriage and career.

The fifth need of children is the mutual respect and attention of their parents. Parents need to be good listeners. They should never be totally focused on their own concerns and agendas. They must not fail to listen to the opinions and concerns of their children.

Each child has a different personality; they must be loved as individuals and molded in positive ways. John Maxwell rightly said, "Our job as parents isn't to force our children into a mold of our own making ... We need to find out who they are and respect them for being who God created them to be."

Parents are blessed when a grandparent chooses to pray for and give spiritual guidance to their grandchildren. A godly grandparent can have a special bond of love for their grandchildren. This bond can help reinforce godly character traits taught by their parents.

When my daughters were in college, my mother made each girl a beautiful golden liberty bell. The bell had a place inside to include this letter:

Dearest Granddaughter,

The Liberty Bell is a symbol of freedom. Freedom from the shackles of sin is my prayer for you. The solution of true freedom is this: "Ye shall know the truth and the truth shall make you free." The truth is found in God's Word. In the Bible, it is written, "Trust in the Lord with all your heart and lean not on your own understanding, but in all your ways acknowledge Him and he shall direct your path" (Proverbs

3:5–6). When you let God direct your path, you will have real freedom. His freedom gives peace and joy.

I will daily think and pray for you as you seek higher wisdom. I would like to add several verses you will find helpful as you seek wisdom.

Reverence and fear of God are basic in all wisdom. Knowing God results in every other kind of understanding. Proverbs is the book of wisdom. I read a chapter in Proverbs every day of the week. This is in addition to my other Bible readings.

If you get troubled, upset, and need perfect calm, meditate on Psalm 23. "The Lord is my shepherd; I shall not want." Meditation on this verse will give you the same peace it gives me.

Don't try to solve problems until you think clearly and can act wisely. I would add, pray about your problems. "A man is a fool to trust himself. But those who use God's wisdom are safe" (Proverbs 28:26).

It is because I love you so much, I'm passing these "goodies" to you.

Love,
Grandmother

The old, yellowed copy of a prayer by Garey Myers saved by my mother shows how parents need to respect and love their children:

Heavenly Father, make me a better parent!
Teach me to understand my children, to listen patiently to what they have to say, and to answer all their questions kindly;
Keep me from interrupting them, talking back to them, contradicting them.
Make me as courteous to them as I would have them to be to me;
Give me the courage to confess my sins against them, and to ask them for forgiveness when I know I have done them wrong;
May I not vainly hurt the feelings of my children;

Forbid I should laugh at their mistakes or resort to scorn and
 ridicule as punishment
Let me not tempt my child to lie or steal;
So guide me hour by hour that I may demonstrate by all I say
 and do that honesty produces happiness.
Reduce, I pray, the meanness in me; may I cease to nag, and when
 I am our of sorts, help me, O Lord, to hold my tongue;
Blind me to the little errors of my children, and help me to see
 the good things that they do—give me a ready word for
 honest praise;
Help me to grow up with my children, to treat them as those of
 their own age, but let me not expect of them the judgment
 and conventions of adults.
Allow me not to rob them of opportunity to wait upon themselves,
 to choose and to make decisions.
Forbid that I should ever punish them for my selfish satisfaction,
May I grant them all their wishes that are reasonable and have
 the courage always to withhold a privilege which I know
 will do them harm;
Make me so fair and just, so considerate and companionable to
 my children that they will have genuine esteem for me;
Fit me to be loved and invited by my children.
With all these gifts, Oh Heavenly Father, give me calmness and
 poise and self-control. Amen.

The sixth need of children is prayer. Parents must choose to pray
with and for their children daily. Children need to see their parents'
dependence on God's guidance. Daily prayers with the reading of
God's Word will build strong families.

Parents can influence their children's choices and behavior in
positive ways by reading the great stories in the Bible. For example,
the story of Daniel and his resolve to serve God while he was held
captive in a heathen land helps children to see the importance of
loving and obeying God. The story of Daniel is only one of many
which can help children develop godly character traits.

Parents must pray faithfully with love and hope for their children. It is important for parents to realize that their children's lives are in the hands of a sovereign God. A parent's prayers will be answered for the good and best interest of their children. Life becomes easier when the parents accept God's sovereign power in the lives of their children.

The fact of God's sovereign power over your children's lives becomes even more apparent when they become teenagers. Older children will have more freedom and peer pressure. When these new freedoms are granted, parents have to trust God and pray for Him to keep their children in his protective care. Parents need to have loving control during these transitional years.

When my girls were teenagers, my Mother sent me a copy of an article from *The Anderson Independent* newspaper dated May 9, 1970, titled, "I Had the Meanest Mother in the World!" The article had originally been published in *Grand Island Independent*.

As a child, I had the meanest mother in the world—she was real mean!

When other kids ate candy for breakfast, she made me eat cereal, eggs, and toast.

When other kids had Coke and candy for lunch, I had to eat a sandwich.

As you can guess, my dinner, too, was different from other kids'.

My *mother* insisted on knowing where we were at all times.

You'd think we were on a chain gang.

She had to know who our friends were—and what we were doing. She insisted that if we said we'd be gone for an hour that we would be gone for one hour or less. She was real mean.

I am ashamed to admit it, but she actually had the nerve to break the child labor laws. She made us work!

We had to wash the dishes, make all the beds, learn to cook, and all sorts of cruel things.

I believe she lay awake at nights thinking up mean things for us to do.

She always insisted on us telling the truth—the whole truth and nothing but the truth.

By the time we were teenagers, she was much wiser, and our life became even more unbearable.

None of this tooting the horn of a car for us to come running. She embarrassed us to no end by making our dates come to the front door to get us.

I forgot to mention, while my friends were dating at the mature age of twelve and thirteen, my old-fashioned mother refused to let me date until I was fifteen or sixteen. She was mean!

My mother was a complete failure as a mother.

None of us has ever been arrested ... or beaten a mate.

Each of my brothers served his time in the service of his country ... willingly, no protesting.

"And whom do we have to blame for this terrible way we turned out? You're right ... our mean mother!

Look at all the things we missed.

We never got to take part in a riot, never burned draft cards, or got to do a million and one things our friends did.

Our mean mother made us grow up into God-fearing, educated, honest adults.

Using this as a background, I am trying to raise my children.

I stand a little taller and I am filled with pride when my children call me mean.

You see ... I thank God he gave me the meanest mother in the world.

An adult child who realized her mother was much smarter than she once believed had written the article.

A mother's love and guidance are the main factors for raising successful adults. Abraham Lincoln, the sixteenth president of the

United States, once said, "All that I am or hope to be I owe to my mother."

Love's influence never ends. When children are grown, they may no longer seek our advice, but they still seek our love. As parents, our love for our children never ends!

Divorce

The best way to avoid having to choose divorce over marriage is to marry the right person. There are many choices in life. The choice of a marriage partner is the second most important decision you make in life. It was said, "Don't look around for a life partner—look up."

In the 21st century, marriage and the family have been strongly attacked by a secular, worldly culture. Statistics show that every other marriage can be expected to fail. What is so shocking is that the rate of success for Christian and non-Christian marriages show very little difference, statistic-wise.

The question arises—why are Christian marriages failing as often as non-Christian unions? The attitude toward marriage today is different from earlier generations. Today, many young couples enter marriage with the attitude, "If it doesn't work out, we can always get a divorce." The commitment is not there, because the godly moral and ethical foundations have become unimportant. Without the moral and ethical foundations, a commitment will lack the strength to survive.

Couples who think they can always get a divorce are thinking only about themselves and their happiness. They are not mature enough to realize the horrible consequences produced by divorce. Divorce can cause feelings of failure, emotional depression, and guilt.

Couples with children have even more difficulties when they decide to terminate their marriage. In addition to difficult custody battles, the children exhibit more emotional problems. Some of the children have problems in school. Others have problems with their relationships. Children can even feel responsible for the divorce. After a divorce, some children suffer financially when raised by a single parent.

Years after children are grown, they can sometimes wrestle with the sadness of their childhood memories of growing up divided between parents on weekends, holidays, and vacations.

Only couples who desire to make the sacrifices necessary to ensure their spouses' happiness over their own should commit to marriage.

Divorce shatters lives, and must be avoided if at all possible.

In order to avoid divorce, you must look for the main reason marriage fails. The main cause for marital failure is *communication.* Lack of communication before or after a marriage can set a couple up for failure. The couple must discuss and mutually agree on the major issues of finance, responsibilities, children, church preference, and goals in life.

Communication about finances is critical to marital success. Finances must be discussed realistically. A budget needs to be made together. How much money will be available to them each month? Will there be enough money to provide adequate food, shelter, clothing, medical care, and (if necessary) child care? How much money, if any, will be left for fun activities and contributions to church and charities? Will there be enough money to save for emergencies? A balanced budget should be able to handle these needs for a family.

After the budget is made, there should be discussion about who will be providing the income. Will both work, or will one be able to stay at home? If there is an option to stay home, is that the desire of the person offered the option? Some women with careers do not plan to stay home. Some men are not comfortable with a wife who prefers to work outside the home. Of course, there are some women who do not want to work outside the home. They want to be home with their children. These questions should be discussed before marriage and end in mutual agreement. Agreement on these questions can help prevent major conflicts later.

Communication regarding children can also cause disagreements. The first decision to be made is whether they both want children. Some couples decide in the beginning not to have children. A major conflict can occur if one of the couple wants a child and the other does not wish to have offspring.

Medical reasons can sometimes cause an inability to produce a child. Also, there could be certain genes in the family that cause the couple to fear having a biological child. If some of these reasons exist, the couple needs to decide if they would agree to adopt. Whatever the decision, the couple must agree about children.

Another area of communication which needs to be addressed is church preference. The couple needs to be completely honest with each other. Problems can arise if one member decides to join a church with the other before marriage and then after marriage and children decides to return to their original church with or without their family. Conflict is greater when children are torn between parents and their churches. When neither parent will compromise, the family is divided.

Communication needs to include a serious talk about goals in life. Goals in life determine how a couple relates to one another. It is important to have the same goals in life. The couple needs to talk about these goals. Will the love for family take preeminence over love for power, success, and fame?

There should be a balance between family and success. Make sure the desire and ambition to support the family is an important goal. The goal should be to take care of the family's needs and have some money left to supply some of their wants. A spouse who just wants to get by in providing for their family is not going to provide an atmosphere for a healthy marriage. A spouse who is willing to work hard to give their family the best they can give them will have the love and respect of their family.

Couples who are mutually committed to bringing glory to God through their marriages should be godly parents and good neighbors, serving those in need within the church and within the community. These couples will have less conflict and will have happier marriages.

Couples must keep their communication skills in use in order to avoid serious conflicts from occurring within their marriage. Lack of honesty in their relationship can cause divorce.

Unfortunately, there are some marriages which cannot be saved. Divorce must occur to prevent further harm to the couple and any children born into the marriage.

What are some causes which prevent a marriage from being saved?

1. A marriage in which adultery has broken the sacred marriage vows and the injured spouse cannot live with the betrayal of the other partner. Adultery is the only Biblical grounds for divorce.
2. A marriage entered into with a deceptive partner—specifically, a heterosexual person who unknowingly marries a gay man or a lesbian woman.
3. Desertion of a spouse for more than a year without the injured person knowing the location of the other.
4. Abuse and violence in a marriage. In the Revised Standard Bible, this verse in Malachi 2:16 says, "'For I hate divorce,' says the Lord God of Israel, 'and the covering one's garment with violence,' says the Lord of Hosts." God hates violence in marriage. Men and women who abuse each other physically or verbally should not remain married. Children should not remain in homes were they are abused by one or both parents.

The Christian church has been forced to deal with the epidemic of divorced church members. The church is making some progress in offering premarital counseling to those wishing to marry. They can attend sessions with a church counselor or the minister. Some of these sessions include compatibility tests, and the couple can discuss their differences and similarities. Certain couples are told to reconsider marriage to each other if the differences would make their marriage a struggle. The old saying, "an ounce of prevention is worth a pound of cure," is certainly true in dealing with insurmountable differences between couples.

In addition to premarital counseling, some churches offer seminars to help improve existing marriages. These seminars are offered periodically. The purpose of these sessions is to help couples improve their existing marriages. They are given skills to enrich their marriages.

Divorce is a disappointment and a heavy burden to bear. In the September 8, 1982 *Presbyterian Journal,* an unknown person wrote the following article about the pain of a divorced Christian. The author, whose name is withheld, writes:

> The heaviest burden that a divorced Christian has to bear is not the weight of the world's opinion, but that of church leaders and laymen alike.
>
> Far too often, divorce leads to a total alienation from the church or a quarantine. It's as though an invisible line had been drawn, and the one thing which puts a person behind that line is not the lack of a saving relationship with Christ, but the sin of divorce—no matter whose fault or how severe the battle going on in the heart of the divorced person. But does God draw a line across which his grace cannot flow? Is the free gift of life in Jesus Christ, who suffered and died for all sinners who come to Him in repentance and faith, withdrawn from the person who has been divorced?"
>
> Is this sin of such a different kind that the sinner must be made to suffer as much as possible, for as long as possible, in as many politely excruciating ways as possible, before God's people are willing to erase the line or lift the quarantine?
>
> Is there really anyone who, in the matter of marital relations, and whether separated or together, has a right before God to cast the first stone?

The pain of divorce was so vividly described by this unknown person.

Churches today are helping with the pain, disappointment, and frustration of those going through divorce. Without the love and grace of God's church, these people feel isolated. The Church, of all institutions, must show compassion to those who are hurting and alone.

The Church, through the love Christ, can show these brokenhearted people how to heal and feel loved once again. Christ can give them a whole new heart. They can feel the promises of Christ love. He has promised to never leave or forsake his own. Faith in Christ makes the divorced person feel whole again.

Choice of a Career

Career choice is one of life's major decisions. It is important to make the best possible choice the first time. Careers can be changed if a wrong choice is made. In fact, if you are very unhappy, you should consider another option. For example, in my own life, my parents encouraged me to take business courses the first two years in college. What a miserable two years! A career in business did not fit my abilities, personality, or interests. The lesson learned from this error in judgment was important. Parents, relatives, and friends can encourage certain career choices, but the final decision must be based on one's ability and interests.

Today, as a student in high school, the guidance counselor can help identify the best choices. The counselors are trained to give tests to measure and identify a student's strengths and weaknesses. These tests can be used to indicate which career a student would most likely be more suited to.

One way to observe and gain firsthand experience in a career of interest is by working after school and on weekends.

There are many examples of workplaces which can give a student an idea of the work required for certain careers. For example, if a student would like to be a pharmacist, they should work at a drug store. To explore a career in government, consider being a page at the State House. A career in medicine could be observed from working in nursing homes, hospice, or hospitals. An interest in a law career could be gained by working in an attorney's office. Another good way to see how the law works is to visit the courthouse and witness a trial.

A second way to gain experience and information about a possible career choice is to do volunteer work within the community. The Red Cross, hospice, YMCA, mental health clinic, nursing homes, day care centers for children and older adults, the Salvation Army, hospitals, and churches are ways to observe opportunities in careers that can serve others.

A third way to explore a career possibility is to talk to someone who is presently working or retired from a career. Interview them, and ask questions about the pros and cons of their career choice. Talking with a career person can give you a better understanding of the actual career requirements. They also have hands-on experience working with the people within the workplace environment. After carefully matching abilities, personality traits, and interest with a particular career, one can make a wiser choice.

Happiness Is a Choice

Happiness does not depend on one's circumstances. Happiness depends on the attitude of a heart. Circumstances cannot be changed, but the heart can be changed. Only a contented heart can bring happiness and joy.

The Apostle Paul endured all kinds of pain and hardships. Paul said changing circumstances would not bring contentment, because contentment is a matter of the attitude of the heart.

In Philippians 4:12, Paul did not say he had found a way to change his circumstances so they would be more pleasing to him. He said, "I have learned the secret of being content in any and every situation, whether well fed or hungry, whether living in plenty or want." In Philippines 4:13, he gives us the formula: "I can do everything through Him who gives me strength." With God, all things are possible. Nothing is too hard for God! What exactly is Paul saying? Happiness and a contented heart are only gained by complete trust in God.

In order to have a contented heart, some questions must be asked, such as: Is God in control of my life? Do I trust Him? Do I believe God always has my best interest at heart? In other words, do I believe God is God, God is good, and God always does what's best for his children?

When a heart knows the Creator God who loves unconditionally, a person will be able to accept God's sovereign power over their life. A contented heart will exist when complete trust in God exists.

God can turn bad circumstances into good for the believers who trusted Him. The story of the life of Job proves that God had Job's best interest at heart. God allowed Job to lose his wealth, all his children, and his health.

Job was obedient to God and praised Him throughout all his trials and horrible circumstances. God tried Job's faith, and Job was steadfast in trusting his providence to God's wisdom. Job had a heart which was contented in good times and bad. God was pleased with Job's faithfulness and trust in Him. God restored all Job had lost twofold. Children, wealth, and health were all given to his faithful servant, Job.

The life of Joseph is another example of God's master plan to bring good out of bad circumstances. Joseph's life had a dramatic turn. He went from being the favored son of his father to being a slave in Egypt. God removed Joseph from his family and placed him as second-in-command in Egypt. During a horrible famine, Joseph was able to secure food and save his family from starvation.

The Apostle Paul endured many trials. While in prison, Paul was heard singing and praising God. God used Paul's prison time to witness and convert the jailer. The guard saw Jesus in Paul's life and asked how he could be saved. Jail time was turned from a bad experience to a time of great rejoicing over the jailer's salvation.

Like the great men and women in the Bible endured trials and bad circumstances, everyone will have periods in their own lives when they will be tested with trials and bad circumstances. During these times, it is important to quiet the questions of "if only," "what if," and "why me?" Instead of questioning God's purpose, remember that God uses these trials to work for our good and his glory.

In the King James Bible, James 1:2 says, "We are to count it all joy, when trials come into our lives." Trials are what God uses to give us godly character. For believers, every trial is assigned a divine task. The divine task assigned is to help mold the believer.

I had an experience with this at a Beth Moore retreat. Beth Moore used the book of James to demonstrate how trials are used in positive ways to bring joy in my life. She suggested I should consider my life as a masterpiece of God. God has chosen me and given me one life to live. My life is like a canvas on which the various events of my life are painted. The canvas of my life begins with the blackness of original sin. When I accept Jesus as my Savior, my canvas is filled with light. My life has multiple seasons. Each season of my life is colored by multicolored trials. These trials are the unplanned and undesirable times. The multiple colors added to my canvas during these times helps my life to bloom into a beautiful masterpiece. The masterpiece showing the beautiful colors of my life is the gift I give back to God. When I endure the trials with trust in God and give praise and worship to Him, the angels in heaven are cheering me on!

In our time of trials, we must learn to think on the goodness of our lives. We must literally count our blessings. We are told to count our trials as joy. John Blanchard says, "Joy is the natural outcome of the Christian's obedience to the revealed will of God."

Christians who believe in Romans 8:28 are confident that the verse is true. The verse says, "And we know that all things work together for good to them that love God, to them who are the called according to his purpose." When this truth is in the heart of the believer, they will exhibit peace and hope—even in troubling times. This peace and hope will be a witness to non-Christians.

If someone asks you the source of the hope and confident peace they see in your life during trials, be ready to give them the secret of your heart. The Bible says in 1 Peter 3:15, "But sanctify the Lord in your heart: and be ready always to give an answer to every man that asketh you a reason of the hope that is in you with meekness and fear." The answer to the question of your hope is found in Nehemiah 8:10: "The joy of the Lord is your strength."

Dr. Shelton Sanford, senior pastor of Westminster Presbyterian Church in Rock Hill, South Carolina, gave this formula in a sermon to the congregation one Sunday. The formula for a contented heart and happiness is to believe that *God is God, God is good,* and *God always knows what's best for his children.*

There are some famous quotes about happiness:

"God cannot give us happiness and peace apart from Himself, because it is not there. There is no such thing" (C. S. Lewis).

"Happiness is neither within us only, or without us; it is the union of ourselves with God" (Blaise Pascal).

"He who forgets the language of gratitude can never be on speaking terms with happiness" (C. Neil Strait).

Abraham Lincoln said, "Most people are as happy as they want to be."

Choice of Friendships

Friendships must be wisely chosen. Look for friends who show godly character. Ask God to give you wisdom in choosing friends who love Him and who seek his truth. You will have many casual friends, but only a few close friends. You will spend more time in the presence of these friends; therefore, it is very important they share your love for God. These loyal friends are gifts from God. God gives us close friends to enrich our lives and make our lives happier.

What are the godly character traits to look for in a friend? A godly friend will have received the fruits of the Spirit when they trusted Jesus. Galatians 5:22 lists the qualities to look for in close friends. These qualities are love, joy, peace, patience, kindness, goodness, and self-control.

I do not recall the source of these definitions given below which can help a person choose their friends.

Choose friends who have these qualities:

1. *Love*—Love for God, for others, and themselves.
2. *Joy*—Choose a friend who has joy—one who is thankful and gives praise to God. A friend who has joy has a positive attitude. Put your sneakers on and run from a person with a negative attitude!
3. *Peace*—Choose friends who are at peace with God and themselves. They try to live peaceably with others. They do not cause strife.

4. *Patience*—Choose friends who are willing to wait for the right time. They do not push others into making unwise decisions.

5. *Kindness*—Choose friends who treat others as they wish to be treated.

6. *Goodness*—Choose friends who practice good deeds rather than things that are evil.

7. *Faithfulness*—Choose friends who are faithful to obey God's laws. Choose friends who are trustworthy and loyal.

8. *Gentleness/Meekness*—Choose friends who are humble. Their pride is kept in check by humility. Pride causes arrogance and prejudice. The best safeguard against meanness is humility.

9. *Self-Control*—Choose friends who control their tempers. A self-controlled person will treat his body as a temple of God. They will not use drugs or be involved in sex without marriage.

In addition to these godly character traits, you should choose friends who build your self-steam, share your joys, and give encouraging words in times of disappointment and sadness.

Friendships should involve both giving and taking. Beware when the friendship is one in which one person is always the giver and the other is always the taker.

Choose friends who will stand up for what is right and be willing to defend others who are fighting for the right reasons.

Solomon, in the book of Proverbs, says to avoid friends who devise wicked plans and cause evil to prosper. Remember, friends have the potential to influence behavior for good or evil. People tend to judge others by their friends. Oliver North rightly said on national TV, "Half your life is going to be defined by the company you keep." The old saying, "birds of a feather flock together," is still true today. Another reason not to associate with evil friends is because they will cause wrong thoughts and actions. Evil friends cause sorrow and pain.

Be sure to choose friends who share your common values and morals. These are the kinds of friends who will share memories that will last over time.

Aristotle wrote, "A genuine friend is someone who wants what's good for you and loves you for who you are, not for what you might do in return." When you find a genuine friend, you have found a treasure worth keeping.

The best friend anyone can have is Jesus. He gives us the gifts of truth, beauty, friendship, love, and laughter in our lives. In the Gospels, we see the life of Jesus. Love has always been in God's heart for us, but in Jesus, his love appeared. God revealed himself in Jesus, who is our kind and merciful friend.

The song "What a Friend we have in Jesus" shows the faithfulness of Jesus to us, his children. Jesus is described as the friend who never leaves or forsakes us. In times of grief, troubles, and discouragement, Jesus is always there to hear us when we pray. During these hard times, Jesus comforts and guides us. Jesus gives us peace. We can cast all our cares on Him. In the Bible, Peter, who was an apostle of Jesus, says in 1 Peter 5:7, "Casting all your anxiety upon Him, because he cares for you."

We know Jesus sacrificed his life to save us from our sins. We remember the Bible verse, John 15:13: "Greater love has no man than this, that one lay down his life for his friends." What a friend we have in Jesus!

Someone said, "Our dearest friend is but a shadow compared to Jesus." This is certainly a truth in all believers' hearts.

Choose a Healthy Body

God has given us the ability to choose how we care for our bodies. He has fearfully and wonderfully made us unique. We are made in his image. St. Augustine said, "For a great thing truly is man, made after the image and similitude of God, not as respects the mortal body in which he is clothed, but as respects the rational soul by which he is exalted in honor above the beasts."

The human body is composed of three separate parts. There is the physical body itself, the mind, and the soul. In order to have a healthy physical body, we must also take care and nurture our minds and our souls.

In today's society, we are fortunate to have access to scientific studies which show us how to take care of our physical bodies. One way to take care of our bodies is to choose healthy foods. Studies have proved a good breakfast complete with fiber and protein will help prevent being excessively hungry during the day. A good breakfast can curb the desire to snack or pick up quick foods. Eating a healthy breakfast can help prevent weight gain. Breakfast is the most important meal of the day. Eating a healthy breakfast is the way to start a new day. Never skip breakfast, because it gives the body energy to do its best work.

In addition to a good breakfast, medical evidence shows we can prevent many serious illnesses by limiting our intake of fats and sugars. Studies show we should include more fresh fruits and vegetables, lean meats, and lower-fat dairy products in our diets.

A healthy diet requires discipline in our "hurry up" lifestyles. Fast foods are so tempting. We struggle to resist the quick meals of fried foods and foods with high sugar content offered to us so freely at fast food restaurants. There will be times when we will lose the struggle, and we will go to these fast food eateries. When we do go, we should choose the healthier choices offered. More importantly, choose not to be a regular customer. Choose to prepare healthier meals at home. Working mothers will have to prepare and freeze meals in advance in order to resist eating out or having home delivery.

Moderation is another discipline we need to practice when eating. The Bible tells us not to be gluttons. Overeating causes weight gain. We need to maintain the average weight for our body in order to function at top performance. Obesity causes many unwanted health problems.

We must choose to exercise. Exercise helps give us healthier bodies. Studies show we need to exercise at least thirty minutes daily. Brisk walking has proved to be just as effective as working out on expensive machines or running marathons. Daily exercise is important to maintain a healthy weight and to help promote good benefits to our heart, lungs, and metabolism.

Proper sleep habits are an important choice we need to make. We need to have a regular time set up for sleep each night and adhere to a pattern of getting seven to eight hours of sleep every night. We do not think as clearly or feel as well when we do not get the proper rest at night. Proper rest will let our bodies perform at their best.

We must choose not to abuse our bodies. Abuse of drugs and other mind-altering substances will affect our bodies in negative ways. Alcohol is one of the most abused drugs in America. Beware of the widespread use and the lack of moderation in young and old alike. In order to have a healthy body, never let drugs or alcohol control your body.

Choose not to allow your body to be abused by body piercing and tattoos. These body piercings could cause skin problems. Tattoos can even become an embarrassment in later years. To have tattoos removed can be very expensive.

The Bible tells us we are to keep our bodies pure and holy. In order to keep our bodies pure and holy, we must choose to abstain from sex until marriage. Uncurbed sexual desires and lusts can cause much anxiety and unhappiness. Sexually transmitted diseases and even death can occur when a bad choice is made.

Our mind is an important part within our body. We need to keep our mind healthy. Paul wrote these words in Philippians 4:8: "Whatsoever is true, whatever is honorable, whatever is right, whatever is pure, whatever is lovely, whatever is of good repute, if there is any excellence and if anything worthy of praise, let your mind dwell on these things." In Philippians 4:9, God promises if we practice these qualities, we will have peace with Him.

Today's culture does not promote a mind-set which will provide peace with God. We must choose not to be part of a society in which "anything goes." Every day we are exposed to a media blitz which promotes greed, "me first," sex, porn, lies, and other terrible morals.

In order to have a healthy mind, we must take control over our thoughts and words. When we encounter those things which are evil and godless, we must resolve not to dwell on those things. We must choose God's way as stated in Philippians and dwell on those thoughts, which are true, honorable, and right. God's way of using our mind brings health to our body.

All of our bodies house a soul. God breathed into our bodies his spirit and gave us a soul. St. Augustine described the soul as "a special substance endowed with reason." The soul is the part of our body which gives us our thoughts, will, and the feelings of our hearts.

Our soul gives us the ability to choose to love, worship, and commune with and praise God. When we choose to obey God's will in our life, our soul will have peace in our bodies.

Christians believe our souls are the part of the body which lives after death. Christ broke the curse of death and gave us eternal life through his death and resurrection.

Christians also believe our souls will be judged by God Himself at the end of the world. Those who have lived a life of obedience to

God on earth will have their souls go back to live eternally with God in heaven. Those who rejected God's gift of eternal life through his Son Jesus will have souls which will be doomed to the inconceivable punishment of Hell. The choice is ours!

Choose to Be a Good Steward

The fundamental truth is everything we touch belongs to God. He owns all things. Psalms 24:1 says, "The earth is the Lord's; and all it contains, the world, and those who dwell in it." Psalms 89:11 says, "The heavens are thine; the world and all it contains, thou hast founded them."

God by his grace has called us to be faithful stewards. We are to be his representatives on earth. We have been entrusted to take care of his possessions in such a way that he will be honored and glorified.

Stewardship is important. Seventeen out of thirty-six of Jesus' parables had to do with property and stewardship.

God has given us the gifts and abilities to be good stewards. We have the ability to choose to follow Christ's example in serving as good stewards of all we have been given. In addition to gifts and abilities, believers have the Holy Spirit to guide them in being good stewards.

We must be good stewards, because we will be held responsible to God for our use of the gifts and abilities given to us. After our time on earth, we will die. After our death, we will all appear before the judgment seat of God. We will give an account of our work here on earth. The Bible says in Corinthians 5:10, "For we must all appear before the judgment seat of Christ, that each one may be recompensed for the deeds in the body, according to what he has done, whether good or bad."

What areas of stewardship have been entrusted to us?

1. We have been given the responsibility to rule over all creation.
2. We will give an account of our time and money.
3. Our relationships with others will be judged.
4. We are stewards of the Gospel. Our stewardship involves sharing the Good News with others.

The first area of stewardship is the responsibility to rule over the entire creation. Our job is to represent God and to oversee his entire creation. We are to protect the earth's soil, air, vegetation, trees, natural resources, and all living animals.

The second responsibility of our stewardship is our time. God has given each of us the gift of time on earth. Our time on earth is not by accident. We are here because God put us here. Our life begins when we were conceived and formed in our mother's womb. Death ends our time on earth.

God has given us all equal time. We all have the same amount of time in a day. Nobody has the power to change the date, hour, minute, second, month, or year. Time cannot be stored for future use. Yesterday is gone forever. We must use today wisely. We cannot complain about the lack of time. John Wesley and Alexander the Great only had twenty-four hour days!

How we use our time is our choice. We must choose to make wise use of our time. Our lives here on earth are indeed short. The Bible refers to our lives as "a vapor which appears, and then is gone" (James 4:14). Job 8:9 says our days "upon earth are a shadow." We cannot do everything we want to do in our lifetime. However, we will live long enough to accomplish everything God intends us to do!

There are two ways we can choose to use our time. We can choose to use our days selfishly and squander the precious gift of time, or we can use our time to make the world a better place to live.

When we choose to make the world a better place to live, we can follow Christ as a role model. Christ came to serve and love others.

Christ washed the feet of his disciples. We too must have a servant's heart. Just as no task was too menial for Christ, we must humble ourselves to serve and love others. Service and love for others honor and glorify God.

God has entrusted to us the stewardship of money. When we say "I believe," we have the motivation to be good stewards. When we believe, our hearts are filled with gratitude for the grace of Jesus and his forgiveness to us. We also remember that our Lord Jesus left the riches of heaven to come into the world to live in poverty so we might become rich.

God only asks us for a tenth of our money as a tithe. The Bible tells us in Malachi 3:10, "'Bring the whole tithe—test me in this,' says the Lord Almighty, 'and see if I will not throw open the flood gates of heaven and pour out so much blessing that you will not have room enough for it.'"

After the death of my mother, I found a typewritten page giving her own testimony about tithing. At the top of the page she had used these Bible verses from Malachi 3:8–10 as her reference. Malachi was a minor prophet in the Bible. I would like to quote her feelings about tithing: "God is love. Love is the key that fits life, love of God, and our fellow man. God gave us the Bible because he knew we would need to find the answers to all our problems and we would need it as a guide to live our lives in obedience to Him. It is the only book that will always be up-to-date. Everybody doesn't know about God or the Word of God. The way the Gospel is to be spread throughout the world is by Christians giving a tenth of their wealth back to God. God knew how hard times would be and how it is so human to have a streak of selfishness, so he only asks one dime out of a dollar, and if you had a whole one hundred dollars, he says, 'You keep ninety dollars and just give me ten.'"

In the next paragraph, she says, "I missed out on a lot of blessings because I didn't start tithing until I was fifteen. I was in a play about tithing at a citywide Baptist Training Union meeting at our church. In the first scene, my girlfriend and I were in college, and we were talking about tithing. I told her I had decided to be a tither, and she said she wasn't about to tithe.

"In the second scene, we were old ladies (they powdered our hair and we wore 'grandmother' clothes). We were talking about our lives since college days. My children had all turned out well, and life had been very happy. Her life had been quite different. There were divorces among her children, and there had been some drunkards, and in general her life had been sad. She admitted she regretted not tithing during her college years."

In the following paragraph, she related how she began to tithe at age fifteen. She writes, "The only income I had was fifty cents a week for lunch at school. For fifty cents, you could get a bowl of soup with all the crackers you wanted and a pint of milk. I decided I could do without milk two days a week and have ten cents to put in my envelope on Sunday. I would have been ashamed to put just a nickel in church. But oh, the blessings that began to come my way after I began tithing, and how much more personal God became to me. My prayers were answered, and God showed me he was even interested in my smallest requests. There was a time I was afraid I had failed my algebra exam. I was good in all my subjects except math. I just couldn't fail, because I didn't want to disappoint the aunt and uncle who so graciously let me live with them during my school years.

"After the exam was finished and I returned home, I was unable to sleep that night. I prayed over and over that I would make just enough to get by—a D. Lo and behold, when I got my paper back the next day, there was a B on it! God just performed a miracle; that is all. I was shocked, and I was so happy. I was so happy, and I was on the verge of tears—how magnified [were] my blessings!"

In the next paragraph, she says, "After getting my education, I married, and it was a good many years before I began tithing again. You see, my husband did not tithe, and he could not see the importance of giving a tithe. The Bible says not to give unless you can give it willingly, not of necessity, and not grudgingly.

"Two years after our marriage, we lost every earthly possession we had—except each other—by fire. Still, we didn't tithe. More years passed, and I felt the need of working outside the home in order to help the family situation. I prayed for a job, and I received the work I needed to help my family. I have been tithing ever since. My husband watched me lay my tenth aside, week by week, and finally he began doing likewise. We began teaching our children to tithe when they received jobs after school. I was proud of my husband when he said, 'Children, always take out your tenth, and you will never miss it.'"

In the last paragraph, she says, "Just to mention a few blessings that have come our way since we began to tithe—we have had few doctor bills, and all our needs have been met. I've sent our son, Billy, to military school for two years, and I almost have enough to send him the coming year. Something wonderful just happened—just yesterday. I have wanted a pretty bedroom suite for Carolyn's room. It seemed just like a dream, but yesterday we went to Columbia and bought one. It will be paid for when we pick it up in a week or two. My advice to all you children is to always honor God with the tithe, and you will be blessed all your lives."

In the Bible, there are a number of important passages about money. The tithe belongs to God. We are to set aside this small amount to benefit God's kingdom here on earth. Paul says in Hebrews 13:5, "Keep your lives free from the love of money and be content with what you have, because God has said, 'Never will I leave you; never will I forsake you.'" Our contentment comes from trusting God. We must live lives in a godly manner and be content with the money given us. 1 Timothy 6:6 tells us, "For we brought nothing into this world, and we can take nothing out of it." Matthew 6:33 tells us the first priorities of our lives are not things or money. The verse tells us the kingdom of God is to be our main goal in life. We are also promised if we first seek his kingdom and his righteousness, all things will be added to us.

In order to be a good steward of the money God allows us to have, we must honor Him by being generous in sharing with those in need. We must show the world the love of God by using our money to serve and love others.

Stewardship of our relationships is another area God will hold us accountable for after our lives here on earth end. The Bible gives specific ways husbands and wives are to treat each other—with love and respect. Children are to obey and honor their parents. Friends are to be loyal and trustworthy. We are told to love our neighbors as ourselves. Neighbors are not just those who live next to us, but everyone God puts in our paths. The golden rule, found in the Bible, sums up the way we are to treat others. "Do unto others as you would have them to do unto you."

The Gospel is an important part of our stewardship. God has given us the responsibility to proclaim the Good News of the Gospel to the world. The Gospel is God's plan to bring people into a living, vital relationship with Him.

When we understand and believe the grace and forgiveness of our Lord and Savior, Jesus Christ, our grateful hearts will want to share his love and service with others. We will want others to know that Christ made the difference in our lives—and he can make the same changes in their lives. When our lives are radically changed by the truth of the Gospel, it will be impossible to keep our faith silent. We will have a true concern for the salvation of others.

Believers are called to proclaim the goodness of God and to praise and honor Him—the one who called us out of darkness and sin into his marvelous light. The Bible passage given in Matthew 5:16 shows how Christians should live their lives for God. The verse calls Christians to "let your light so shine before men, that they may see your good works, and glorify your Father which is in heaven." Our primary goal in life should be to reflect the likeness of Christ to a lost, sinful world. The way we live should make it easier for others to believe in God's truth and love.

Among my mother's notes was a yellowed copy of a lesson she taught to a group of young people. The lesson was about the importance of living a lifestyle which would be a witness for Christ. The lesson was simply titled "Letters."

The first part of the lesson talked about how the Jews brought letters of recommendation with them from their churches. Paul talked about these letters of recommendation in 2 Corinthians 3. He said he did not need a letter of recommendation, because "you and your changed lives" were the recommendation. "You are a living letter of Christ's love."

The purpose of the lesson was to teach the responsibility of each Christian to proclaim the Gospel by living a life which reflected honor and glory to Him. Each life's "letter" was to be a witness to the lost world. Their letters of recommendation represented six types of lives.

The first letter was hard to read, because the life was so far away from God. The life without prayer and communication with God loses the message of salvation.

The second letter was dim, because the will of God had not been sought. Bible study, prayer, and worship in God's house had been neglected.

In the third letter, the message had gotten so blurred the world could not read it. This life had compromised with the world. Only part of the life and part of the tithe had been given back to God.

The fourth letter does not show the witness of Christ, because it is covered with sinful habits and worldly amusements.

The fifth letter cannot be read, because it is too soiled. There are too many little sins covering the message. They are not big sins, but they hide God's Word. Smutty stories, bad words, and evil deeds have covered up the message.

The sixth letter can be read as a witness for Christ, because this life shows a resolve to not conform to the world, but to live a life dedicated to holy living. In the Bible, we find these words in Romans 12:1—2: "I urge you therefore, brethren, by the mercies of God, to present your bodies a living and holy sacrifice, acceptable to God, which is your spiritual service of worship. And do not be conformed to this world, but be transformed by the renewing of your mind, that you may prove what the will of God is, that which is good and acceptable and perfect." Lives lived in this manner show good stewardship of the Gospel.

What Christians Believe

Christians should choose to know what they believe. All Christians should be able to give an answer to those who ask, "What is your hope?" Remember, those who do not read the Bible are watching the lives of Christians. Christians who reflect the resemblance of Christ's love and grace in their daily lives are sometimes the only witness an unbeliever can see and experience. In order to practice the faith, Christians must know what they believe.

The basic statements in the Apostle's Creed are a good place to confirm your belief as a Christian.

The Apostle's Creed

I believe in God the Father Almighty, maker of heaven and earth; and in Jesus Christ, his only Son, our Lord; who was conceived by the Holy Ghost, born of the Virgin Mary, suffered under Pontius Pilate, was crucified, dead, and buried, he descended into hell. On the third day, he arose again from the dead. He ascended into heaven, and sitteth on the right hand of God the Father Almighty; from thence he shall come to judge the quick and the dead. I believe in the Holy Ghost; the holy catholic church; the communion of saints; the forgiveness of sins; the resurrection of the body; and life everlasting. Amen.

In addition to the Apostle's Creed, there are other basic truths a Christian should know and believe. These include the Ten

Commandments, the greatest commandment, the Beatitudes, the Lord's Prayer, the fruit of the Spirit. Some of the important scripture verses also need to be memorized.

The Ten Commandments were given to Moses as a guide for living an obedient life to God. These commandments are still used by Christians today to direct their lives and choices.

The Ten Commandments

Exodus 20:1–17

1. You shall have no other gods before me.
2. You shall not make for yourself an idol in the form of anything in heaven above or on earth beneath or in the waters below. You shall not bow down to them or worship them; for I, the Lord your God, am a jealous God, punishing the children for the sin of the fathers of the third and fourth generations of those who hate me, but showing love to a thousand generations of those who love me and keep my commandments.
3. You shall not misuse the name of the Lord your God, for the Lord will not hold anyone guiltless who misuses his name.
4. Remember the Sabbath day by keeping it holy. Six days shall you labor and do all your work, but on the seventh day is a Sabbath to the Lord your God. On it you shall not do any work, neither you, nor your son or daughter, nor your manservant or maidservant, nor your animals, nor the alien within your gates. For in six days the Lord made the Heavens and the earth, the sea, and all that is in them, but he rested on the seventh day. Therefore the Lord blessed the Sabbath day and made it holy.
5. Honor your father and mother, so that you may live long in the land the Lord your God is giving you.
6. You shall not murder.
7. You shall not commit adultery.

8. You shall not steal.
9. You shall not give false testimony against your neighbor.
10. You shall not covet your neighbor's house. You shall not covet your neighbor's wife, or his manservant or maidservant, his ox or donkey, or anything that belongs to your neighbor.

The Greatest Commandment

Jesus gave the greatest commandment. Jesus was asked what the greatest commandment was. A Pharisee who was a lawyer was trying to trick Jesus with his question. Jesus replied in Matthew 22:36–40, "Love the Lord your God with all your soul and with all your mind. This is the first and greatest commandment. And the second is like it: Love your neighbor as yourself." Jesus then said, "On these two commandments hang all the law and prophets."

The Beatitudes

The beatitudes can be found in Matthew 5. Jesus gave the beatitudes in the Sermon on the Mount. They were given to serve as a guide for living the obedient life. The following is a list of the eight beatitudes and the meaning of each. The Beatitudes can be called the eight keys to heaven.

Notes on the Beatitudes were taken from Charles Allen's book, *God's Psychiatry*. Some of the explanations of the meanings of the Beatitudes are taken from sermon notes given by my pastor, Dr. Shelton Sanford.

1. "Blessed are the poor in spirit, for theirs is the kingdom of heaven." What does it mean to be poor in spirit? In order to be poor in spirit, you must give up a prideful attitude. You must humble yourself before God and admit to Him that you are a sinner who does not deserve his grace. Admit to God that you cannot buy or work

your way into heaven. The first Beatitude is the most important key to heaven, because without humbling yourself before Christ and accepting his grace and gift of salvation, the other keys to heaven will not be evident in your life. The blessing for being "poor in heart" is admittance into heaven.

2. "Blessed are those who mourn, for they shall be comforted." When you humble yourself before God, you see God's holiness and your hopeless, sinful condition. You mourn over your sins. The blessing is, "they shall be comforted."

3. "Blessed are the meek, for they shall inherit the earth." The third beatitude shows us how to interact with others as believers in Christ. Lloyd-Jones says, "Meekness is essentially a true view of oneself expressing itself in attitude and conduct with respect to others." The Greek adjective, which is translated *meekness,* means "humble, gentle, considerate, and courteous." Just as Jesus provided the perfect example of meekness, you must surrender yourself to the plans and purposes of God. The blessing is, "they shall inherit the earth."

4. "Blessed are those who hunger and thirst for righteousness, for they shall be satisfied." John Stott says, "righteousness in the Bible has at least three aspects: legal, moral, and social." Hungering and thirsting for righteousness means you desire to be free from sin in all its forms. You desire to live a holy life. The blessing is, "they shall be satisfied."

5. "Blessed are the merciful, for they shall receive mercy." Mercy is compassion for other people's needs. You have a desire to relieve the suffering of others. Mercy is paying back good for evil. The blessing is, "they shall receive mercy."

6. "Blessed are the pure in heart, for they shall see God." In order to have a pure heart, you must not be hypocritical. Your heart must be for God alone. Your heart has been

cleansed by Jesus blood on the cross. The blessing is, "they shall see God."

7. "Blessed are the peacemakers, for they shall be called the sons of God." The Bible describes a peacemaker in Romans 12:18 and in Ephesians 4:31–32. A peacemaker desires peace and does all they can to produce peace. A peacemaker wants all people to be at peace with God. The blessing is, "they shall be called the sons of God."

8. "Blessed are those who have been persecuted for the sake of righteousness, for theirs is the kingdom of God." When you are righteous, you are like the Lord. In John 15:18–19, it says, "If the world hates you, you know that it has hated me before it hated you. If you were of the world, the world would love its own; but because you are not of the world, but I chose you out of the world; therefore, the world hates you." You will be persecuted, because you are called to be different from the world. The blessing is, "theirs is the kingdom of heaven."

The Lord's Prayer

Our Father, which art in heaven, hallowed be thy name. Thy kingdom come. Thy will be done, in earth as it is in heaven. Give us this day our daily bread, and forgive us our debts, as we forgive our debtors. And lead us not into temptation, but deliver us from evil. For thine is the kingdom, and the power, and the glory forever. Amen.

The disciples asked Jesus to teach them to pray, and he taught them the Lord's Prayer. This prayer is found in the Bible in Matthew 6:9–13.

The Fruit of the Spirit

The fruits of the Spirit, like the Beatitudes, are guidelines for living the Christian life. The Fruits of the Spirit can be found in Galatians 5:22–23. "But the fruit of the spirit is love, joy, peace, patience, kindness, goodness, faithfulness, gentleness, and self-control."

In a Beth Moore study, she showed how all the qualities are really expressions of the first fruit of the Spirit—love.

Joy is *love* enjoying.
Peace is *love* resting.
Patience is *love* waiting.
Kindness is *love* reacting.
Goodness is *love* choosing.
Faith is *love* believing.
Gentleness is *love* empathizing.
Self-control is *love* resisting temptation.

In addition to the basic truths of Christianity, choose to memorize and meditate on Scripture verses. Jesus quoted scriptures when the devil tempted Him in the wilderness. Christians need to follow Jesus' example and use Scripture in times of need. Scripture can bring comfort, strength, guidance, and joy to lives.

These are a few of the verses that strengthen your faith:

"For God so loved the world that he gave his only begotten Son, that whosoever believeth in Him should not perish but have everlasting life" (John 3:16). This verse is the good news of the gospel. Most Christians memorize this verse when they become believers.

"God is our refuge and strength, a very present help in trouble" (Psalm 46:1).

"Trust in the Lord with all your heart; and lean not unto thine own understanding. In all thy ways acknowledge Him, and he shall direct thy paths" (Proverbs 3:5–6).

"The Lord is near to all who call upon Him, to all who call upon Him in truth" (Psalm 145:18).

"Casting all your anxiety upon Him, because he cares for you" (1 Peter 5:7).

"Like apples of gold in settings of silver is a word spoken in right circumstances" (Proverbs 25:11).

"The angel of the Lord encampeth round about them that fear him, and delivereth them" (Psalm 34:7).

"Fear God and keep his commandments: for this is the whole duty of man" (Ecclesiastes 12:13).

"He has told you, O man, what is good; and what does the Lord require of you but to do justice, to love kindness, and to walk humbly with God" (Micah 6:8).

"The Lord is good, a stronghold in the day of trouble. And he knows those who take refuge in Him" (Nahum 1:7).

"If I should say, 'My foot has slipped,' Thy loving kindness, O Lord, will hold me up. When my anxious thoughts multiply within me, Thy consolations delight my soul" (Psalm 94:18–19).

"For I know the thoughts that I think towards you, saith the Lord, thoughts of peace, and not of evil, to give you an expected end" (Jeremiah 29:11).

"For by grace are ye saved through faith; and that not of yourselves: it is the gift of God. Not of works lest any man should boast" (Ephesians 2:8–9).

"The eyes of the Lord are upon the righteous, and his ears are open to their cry" (Psalm 34:15).

"The Lord shall preserve thee from all evil: he shall preserve thy soul" (Psalm 121:7).

"But they that wait upon Lord shall renew their strength; they shall mount up with wings as eagles; they shall run and not be weary; they shall walk and not faint" (Isaiah 40:13).

"But thou, O Lord, art a shield for me, my glory, and the lifter up of mine head" (Psalm 3:3).

"The eternal God is thy refuge, and underneath are the everlasting arms" (Deuteronomy 33:27).

"Thanks be to God, who gives us the victory through our Lord Jesus Christ" (1 Corinthians 15:57).

"The Lord is my shepherd, I shall not want. He makes me lie down in green pastures; he leads me beside quiet waters. He restores my soul; he guides me in the paths of righteousness for his name's sake. Even though I walk through the valley of the shadow of death, I fear no evil; for Thou art with me; Thy rod and thy staff, they comfort me. Thou dost prepare a table before me in the presence of my enemies; Thou hast anointed my head with oil; My cup overflows, surely goodness and loving kindness will follow me all the days of my life, and I will dwell in the house of the Lord forever" (Psalm 23).

The twenty-third Psalm is one of the most famous Psalms. Christians often recite this Psalm if they are in danger or need reassurance of God's presence with them. This Psalm is often read at funerals.

Choices Made
by Famous Men and Women in the Bible

When we study the choices of famous men and women in the Bible, we realize they had the same sinful nature as we have today. The same temptations still exist. The Bible shows us the realities of life. We see that even the most godly men and women in the Bible made both good and bad choices.

The Bible does not tell us about their sins to weaken our senses of moral alarm, but to help us be on guard morally. When we read and study their weaknesses and failures, it makes us see our own vulnerability and need of God's guidance in our choices.

We can gain insight into making wiser choices by looking at their right and wrong choices. The Bible clearly shows the consequences of their choices. Right choices always brought glory to God and blessings. Wrong choices brought sadness and painful consequences. The lives of these men and women show sin can be forgiven, but the consequences of sin will not be erased and must be endured.

Abraham

The story of Abraham is found in the book of Genesis. Abraham was seventy-five years old when God called him to leave his country and go to a land God would reveal to him. He had to make a choice. Would he stay with his relatives in a comfortable, familiar surrounding, or would he obey God and go to a new land? Abraham made the right choice; he believed God's promise that his descendants would become a great nation. He had faith God had his best interest in mind, and he believed God would be with him and bless him. The Bible says that Abraham was a friend of God. God talked with him and revealed his plans to him. God promised to make his heirs as numerous as the stars.

After many years, Abraham and Sarah were still childless. Abraham even considered Eliezer, the steward of his house, to produce a child for him. God had told Abraham his heir would be from his own bloodline. Abraham and Sarah became anxious for a child. Sarah made a wrong choice by giving her handmaiden, Hagar, to her husband, Abraham, for a wife. When Hagar conceived, Sarah became jealous because she was still barren. She became bitter and was unkind to Hagar. The home situation was so bad, Hagar fled from Abraham's house. She fled to the desert. The angel of the Lord appeared to her and told her she would have a son. The child was to be named Ishmael. The angel told her the son would be the father of a great nation. Ishmael's descendants rightly claim Abraham as their father. Ishmael's descendents are the Arabs today.

After the birth of Ishmael, God made a covenant with Abraham. He promised Abraham he would be the father of a great nation, and Sarah would bear the covenant child. Abraham was 100 years old, and Sarah was ninety! The covenant gave Abraham and the descendents of the covenant the land of Canaan as an everlasting possession. In return, Abraham promised to obey his commandments.

Sarah gives birth to the covenant child, Isaac. God established his everlasting covenant through Isaac and his seed forever. Isaac's descendents are the Jews today.

After Isaac was born, God tested Abraham's faith. God wanted to see if Abraham fully trusted Him to work out the best plan for his life. God told him to take his beloved son up on a mountain and make him a sacrifice to God. Abraham obeyed God, but God did not allow Isaac to be sacrificed. God provided a ram for the sacrifice. Abraham made the right choice to trust God, and the blessing of the covenant was through the covenant child, Isaac.

What can we learn from the choices made by Abraham and Sarah?

1. God chooses who he calls to carry on his work here on earth. God sometimes uses the most unlikely people. Abraham came from a pagan culture which served many gods.
2. Like Abraham, we might be asked to leave our familiar country to serve God.
3. We must be patient with God. God's timing is not always our timing.
4. We must trust God to work all circumstances we encounter for our best interest.
5. We must not try to fix things ourselves. We must be patient with God.

Esther

The story of Esther in the Old Testament is a lesson in obedience and right choices. God used a Jewish orphan held in captivity to accomplish the spectacular task of saving the Jewish people.

Esther was a young Jewish girl in Persia. Mordecai, her uncle, was raising her. Both of Esther's parents were dead. Mordecai loved Esther as his own daughter. She was faithfully trained in the Jewish scriptures.

King Ahasuerus, or Xerxes, ruled over the Persian empire. He was not a wise and God-fearing man, as his father King Darius had been. He was foolish and weak.

After Ahasuerus had been king for three years, he had a huge banquet for all the princes and nobles from each of his provinces come for a party. The party lasted six months! At the end of this party, the king gave a feast for all the people in the capital city of Shushan. The people were divided into two parties. Men and women were separated. In that country, no lady ever came into a room of men without a veil covering her face.

While the king was entertaining the men at their party, Queen Vashti was giving a feast for the women. The party's festivities lasted a week. On the seventh day of the feast, Queen Vashti was summoned to come before a very drunk king. If he had not been so drunk, he would never have asked her to appear before all the men at the party with only the royal crown on her head. She would never put herself in a crowd of men without her face being covered.

Queen Vashti refused to obey the king's command. The king was furious, and he consulted his seven wise men about this act of disobedience. He asked, "What shall be done to Queen Vashti, because she refused to obey the king's command?" The wise men decided the queen should lose her position as Queen of Persia. They advised the king to search for a replacement who would be more obedient to the king.

The king sent out a search party to find the most beautiful virgins in the kingdom. These virgins would be put into the king's harem. He would call them to come before him one night at a time. The one who pleased him the most would be the next Queen of Persia.

Persia was a pagan society and did not value a woman's dignity or worth. The virgins who were not chosen would be the property of the king forever. To be chosen was an honor and would result in a life of luxury. However, if a virgin was not chosen, she would become a number in the king's harem. The virgins in the harem had virtually no contact with the outside world.

Esther was a beautiful virgin. Mordecai must have had feelings of pride, but at the same time, he must have had feelings of despair for her well-being in the care of the king's harem.

Esther was different from the other virgins. She was not self-seeking. She did not ask for jewels and lavish clothing. The virgins could ask for anything they wished to make their entrance before the king as impressive as possible. Esther wore the attire suggested by Hegai, the man in charge of the harem. She trusted his judgment. She had already found favor with Hegai. Hegai made sure Esther's attire would please the king. Esther had impressed Hegai by her manners, unselfishness, and obedience. Esther was beautiful—inside and outside! Hegai was hoping she would be the king's choice.

Esther pleased the king and found favor over all the other virgins. The king was pleased with her physical beauty, but like Hegai, he saw her deeper beauty. The king realized she had a wonderful attitude, she was humble, and she cared about others. What a list of desirable characteristics! He truly loved Esther, and he put the queen's crown upon her head.

Every day, Mordecai walked before the court of the women's house and sat at the palace gate to find out how Esther was. He was able to send messages to Esther while he was at the gate. Mordecai was an official government employee. He was like a member of the king's secret police. He was able to learn the political news of the day while sitting at the gate. While he lingered about the palace, he discovered a plot between two servants to kill King Ahasuerus.

Mordecai got word to Esther about the plot, and she warned the king. The plot was proved, and the two men were hanged. Esther told the king that Mordecai was responsible for giving her the information that saved his life. The act of Mordecai was written in the book of annals in the presence of the king, but no reward was given to Mordecai.

A very evil man named Haman was a favorite of all the king's princes. He was given many privileges and honors other princes did not receive. In fact, all the other servants and princes were required to bow low with their faces to the ground when Haman passed by. He thought himself more important than any one else.

Mordecai alone did not bow down when Haman passed. The servants noticed his insubordination and questioned him. They asked, "Why do you not obey the king's command to bow before Haman?" Mordecai was obeying God's law. Jews did not bow to anyone but God. When he continued not to bow, they told Haman.

Haman was furious. He devised a plan to punish Mordecai. He decided that since Mordecai was a Jew, he would destroy all Jews in the kingdom.

Haman appeared before the king with his plan. He knew the king would not allow him to kill thousands people just because

Mordecai would not bow before him, so he appealed to the king's vanity.

Haman started his speech with praise for the king. He said, "Oh king, live forever! There is a certain group of people who live in your kingdom who have different laws. They do not keep the king's laws. It does not profit the king for them to live. If it pleases the king, I will have them destroyed." He even offered to pay 10,000 talents into the king's treasury so the king would not lose any taxes by having them killed. The king told Haman to keep his silver. He was given permission to do whatever he liked to these people.

The king gave Haman his royal ring with the king's seal on it. Haman now had the power to write anything he wished and sign it with the seal on the king's ring. When it was signed with the king's ring, it would become a law of the Medes and Persians which could not be altered.

Haman gathered all the king's secretaries. He told them to write to each of the governors who ruled over the provinces of the empire and give them this decree from the king. On the thirteenth day of the twelfth month, they were to kill all the Jews—both young and old, little children and women!

When Mordecai heard that all Jews were to be killed, he tore his clothes, put on sackcloth and ashes, and went out into the middle of the city, raising a loud and bitter cry.

Esther did not know about the decree Haman had sent out. Some of her handmaidens, however, told her Mordecai was outside the gates in mourning attire.

Esther sent him some good clothes to wear instead of the sackcloth and ashes. Mordecai sent the clothes back. When the servant brought the clothes back, Esther was confused and wondered what the matter with her uncle was. She sent one of her servants back to ask Mordecai the meaning of the mourning clothing.

Mordecai gave the servant a copy of the decree to show the queen. He asked Esther to go in to the king and beg for the lives of her people.

Esther was afraid when she heard this horrible message. She told the servant to tell Mordecai this rule. Any man or woman who came into the king's inner court without being summoned was almost certain to die. They would be put to death unless the king held out his golden scepter as a sign that they may live. She told the servant to tell Mordecai that she had not been called before the king for thirty days! She did not feel she could go before the king unless he called for her. She could be in grave danger—even though she was the queen!

Mordecai knew the law and the danger she faced, but he knew the Jews were going to be completely destroyed if she did not intervene for them.

Mordecai sent a message back to Esther and warned her not to stand idle and let her people die. He told Esther, "Think not with thyself that thou shalt escape in the king's house, more than all the Jews. For if thou altogether holdest thy peace at this time, then shall their enlargement and deliverance arise to the Jews from another place; but thou and thy father's house shall be destroyed: and who knoweth whether thou art come to the kingdom for such a time as this?"

Esther was terrified when she thought of going into the king without being called. She knew she would need the fasting and prayers of her people. She sent a message to Mordecai asking for all the Jews in the city to fast and pray for three days. She promised she and her maidens would also fast and pray for three days. After the three days were up, she promised to go before the king. She said, "If I perish, I perish!"

After three days, Esther put on her royal robes and stood in the inner court of the palace. Her heart was beating rapidly while she waited for the king to see her. When the king saw his beautiful young queen, he was pleased, and he held out the golden scepter for her to touch.

The king spoke kindly to her. "What do you wish, Queen Esther? What is your request? It shall be given you, even the half of the kingdom."

Esther was afraid to tell him the real reason she had come before him. She wisely invited the king and Haman to a feast which she had prepared for them that day.

The king was very happy with her request. He sent a servant to bring Haman to the banquet. At the banquet, the king asked Esther again what she wanted, for he could tell she had something on her mind.

Esther was still afraid to tell him what was troubling her. She simply said, "If it pleases the king, let the king and Haman come again tomorrow to another banquet, which I shall prepare. Then I will tell the king my request."

Haman was overjoyed at the thought attending another banquet with only the king and queen present. He left feeling quite proud and honored. He had to go by the gate to leave the palace. His joy left him at the sight of Mordecai, because he refused to bow before him.

When Haman went home, he called all his family and friends around him. He bragged about his riches and the honors given to him by the king. After be bragged about his favored position, he said the honors meant nothing to him, because Mordecai would not bow to him. This disrespect made him very angry.

Haman was so disturbed, his wife and friends offered a solution. They said, "Let a gallows be made, seventy-five feet high. After the gallows are made, go to the king and ask permission to hang Mordecai on them. Then you can go to the banquet with the king and the queen with a happy heart."

Haman was pleased with the solution. He had gallows prepared that very afternoon. The thought of Mordecai on the gallows made him very happy.

King Ahasuerus could not sleep the night before the second banquet. He had one of his servants bring the book of records which recorded his reign to him. The servant was asked to read the records to the king. The records showed how Mordecai had uncovered the plot to murder him. Mordecai had saved the king's life! The king asked the servant, "What reward has been given to Mordecai for this?" The servant told the king, "Nothing has been done for him." The king made up his mind to reward Mordecai for his loyal service.

About the time of the servant's conversation with the king, Haman appeared in the outer court to ask the king permission to let him hang Mordecai on the gallows he had built.

The king told the servant to let Haman come in. After Haman came in, the king asked Haman a question: "What shall be done to the man whom the king delights to honor?"

Haman vainly thought he was the man the king wanted to honor. Haman gave the king a list of the things he would want given to honor himself. After giving the list of honors to be placed on the man the king wished to reward, the king told Haman to give all the honors to Mordecai, the Jew!

Haman was devastated. He had felt he was to be given the honor. He could not believe he would be leading the horse Mordecai would be riding through the streets with high honor given by the king.

After the procession that honored Mordecai was over, Haman went home in shame. He told his wife and friends everything that had happened. While he was still talking with them, the king's servant called him to the banquet Queen Esther had prepared.

While they were eating at the banquet, the king again asked the queen her request.

Queen Esther fell on her knees and said, "If I have found favor in your sight, O King, let my life be given to me at my petition and my people's life at my request. For we are sold, I and my people, to be destroyed."

The king had compassion for his beautiful queen, and he became angry at the idea his queen and her people were to be destroyed. The king asked the queen, "Who has dared to do such a thing?" Esther pointed to the evil Haman.

The king arose and walked into the palace garden to cool his anger. While the king was outside, Haman fell on the couch near the queen to beg for his life.

When the king returned to the room and saw Haman so close to the queen, he became very angry. The servants saw the king's anger and realized the king would order Haman to be put to death. They covered his face with a cloth. One of the servants volunteered information about the gallows made for Mordecai, the king's friend.

The king listened to the servant and decided to hang Haman on the gallows he had made for Mordecai.

Esther told the king Mordecai had raised her as his own daughter. After they talked, the king sent for Mordecai and gave him the ring he had given Haman. He made Mordecai the highest officer in all of Persia.

Even though Haman was dead, the decree was still to be carried out according to the law. Therefore, Esther still had work to do. She would have to go back to the king and beg to have the decree changed so the Jews would not be killed.

The king said he could not change the sealed law, but he would give Mordecai permission to send another message to the Jews. The message said on the thirteenth day of the twelfth month, the king gave the Jews permission to organize and fight those who wanted to hurt or kill them.

The Jews overcame all their enemies and hanged the ten sons of Haman.

After the victory was won, the Jews celebrated for two days. The Jews continue to celebrate this victory today to remember when the Jewish race was saved from destruction. The celebration is called the Feast of Purim.

What can we learn from studying the choices in the book of Esther?

1. We need to be obedient and humble in spirit to accomplish God's work on earth.
2. Inner beauty is far more important than physical beauty.
3. We need to be reminded, like Esther, that if we do not obey God and do his will, God can choose someone else. We will miss the blessing.
4. Esther had faith in the providence of God, even in difficult times. We need to have this same faith when our circumstances are not happy.

Daniel

The Bible tells us Daniel was one of the Jewish princes taken into Babylonian captivity by King Nebuchadnezzar. The king wanted these princes to be attendants at his palace.

The master of the king's servants was told to choose only the most intelligent and handsome young men. He wanted them to be endowed with wisdom and understanding. They were to be taught the language and literature of the Chaldeans.

Daniel and three of his friends were chosen for the king's court. These Jewish boys had lived in godly homes. They knew the Scriptures and the laws of Moses. They were secure in their belief that only their God was the God who made heaven and earth. They knew that obedience to God alone brought security and peace to their lives. Daniel resolved in his heart that he would be faithful to God and his direction for his life.

Daniel's right choice in resolving to serve only the one true God, even in the difficult times of captivity, pleased God. God was able to use Daniel for the furthering of his kingdom on earth.

King Nebuchadnezzar took these four young princes into his court to train them in the lifestyle of the Chaldeans. They were to eat the king's meat and drink the king's wine.

Daniel and his three friends did not want to break the laws of his Jewish heritage. The king's meat and the king's wine were unclean for the Jewish boys. Daniel was determined to be faithful to his God's laws.

Daniel went to the master of the servants, who had charge of the food of the young princes. He asked if he and his three friends could be excused from eating the king's meat and drinking the king's wine. God was with them, and the servant was friendly. The servant said he would be glad to excuse them, but he was afraid they might not look as healthy as the other boys, and the king would cut off his head!

Daniel did not give up. He asked if they could just eat vegetables and drink water for a ten-day trial.

The master of servants let them try the diet of vegetables and waters for ten days. After ten days, the four boys were healthier than all the others who ate the king's food and drank his wine.

God was faithful and rewarded these four boys with knowledge and skills. Daniel was given the special ability to have understanding in visions and in dreams.

At the end of three years of training, the princes had been thoroughly taught the Chaldean customs. They were well versed in the literature and language of their new country. The king had even had their names changed from Jewish names to Chaldean names. Daniel's name was changed to Belteshazzar. Hananiah was given the name of Shadrach. Mishael was named Meshach. Azariah was called Abed-nego.

When these four princes came before the king, he found they had ten times more wisdom and knowledge than all the magicians and astrologers in his kingdom.

One night, King Nebuchadnezzar had a strange dream. All the magicians and astrologers were called in to explain the meaning of the dream. These wise men asked the king to tell them his dream.

The king said he had forgotten the dream. He challenged them to tell him the dream and its meaning. If they would not tell them the dream and its meaning, he would cut them into pieces and tear down their houses! If they could tell the dream and its meaning, they would receive valuable gifts and great honor.

The magicians and astrologers were terrified. They answered the king by saying it would be impossible to tell the king his dream, because he did not remember what he dreamed.

The king was furious! He said they were not true wise men. He called his soldiers and ordered them to cut off the heads of the wise men!

The king ordered a search for all wise men in the city. The heads of the magicians, sorcerers, and astrologers were to be cut off. Daniel and his friends were in great danger, because they were considered to be wise men.

When Daniel heard about the dream and the fate of all the wise men, he was brave enough to go before the king unannounced. No one could go before the king without being called. The king held a golden scepter in his hand; if someone entered the room without the king offering his golden scepter, it meant instant death by the king's soldiers.

Daniel knew about this custom. Daniel trusted his God to keep him safe. Daniel bowed low, asked the king to give him time to think, and he would tell the king the dream and its meaning.

The king agreed to wait. Daniel went home. He asked his three friends to pray with him. They prayed God would reveal the dream and its meaning to them so they would not be put to death like the other wise men.

God was faithful. God revealed the dream to Daniel while he was sleeping that night. Daniel thanked God for his kindness to him. Then he went to the captain of the king's soldiers and asked him to take him to the king so he could tell the king his dream and its meaning.

The captain of the king's soldiers was elated. He hurried to inform the king and tell him not to cut off the heads of all the wise men. He told the king one of the captives from Judah could tell him his dream.

Daniel was called before the king. The king asked, "Can you tell me my dream and its meaning?"

Daniel was very humble. He told the king it would be impossible for the magicians and other wise men to tell him a dream he had forgotten. Daniel told the king, "There is a God in heaven who sent a dream to the king to show him what will happen in the future." Daniel said God had not revealed this dream to him because he was smarter than the other wise men, but God revealed the dream to him because He wanted the king to know the meaning behind the dream.

King Nebuchadnezzar was astonished when Daniel told him his dream and the meaning for the future. The king fell down on his face before Daniel and acknowledged that Daniel's god was a "God of gods, a Lord of kings, and a revealer of secrets."

The king was impressed with Daniel. Daniel received many valuable gifts. The king made Daniel ruler over all of Babylon and chief of the governors of the wise men.

Daniel had caused King Nebuchadnezzar to learn of the greatness of the God of the Hebrews, but he still did not acknowledge that Jehovah was the only true God.

Pagan King Nebuchadnezzar still believed that the idol he worshipped had made it possible for him to conquer the nations around him.

The king decided to show his gratitude to the god he worshipped by making a golden image of this god. The image of the god was nine feet high. The image could be seen glittering in the sun for miles around.

The king decided to have all the rulers of the provinces of the kingdom of Babylon come to a dedication service for the image. He made a proclamation that at the sound of all kinds of musical instruments playing, all would be required to fall down and worship the golden image. All who did not obey the king's proclamation would at the same hour be cast into the midst of a fiery furnace.

The three friends of Daniel—Shadrach, Meshack, and Abed-nego—were faithful to their God's law, which forbade them to bow to a graven image.

Daniel's friends were reported to the king by some jealous wise men. Daniel and his friends had favor with the king, and the native Chaldean wise men did not like the Jewish princes who had been given more power than them.

After the wise men told the king about the disobedience of Daniel's friends, the king called them into the court. He gave them one more chance to bow before the image. They told the king they would not bow down. They said their God was able to save them, but if he chose not to save them, they wouldn't bow before the golden image.

The king was very angry at their disobedience to him. He called his soldiers. They bound the men and cast them into the furnace while the king watched. The king was astonished to see not three men in the furnace, but four! He saw they were not burned or hurt, and the fourth man looked like a god. When they were taken from the furnace, they did not even smell of fire.

The king exclaimed the power of the God of the Hebrews. He even commanded this God to be honored everywhere in the kingdom. Many of the heathen Chaldeans began to respect the God of the Jewish princes.

When the Persians took over the Babylonian empire, the empire was so large that King Cyrus put Darius as king over Babylon. King Darius divided his kingdom into many smaller parts, and over these parts he placed princes. Over the princes were three presidents. Daniel was placed over the three presidents.

When Daniel, a Jew, had the chief position, the other princes became jealous. They began to plot some way to get him in trouble. Daniel was so faithful they could not find a fault to accuse him.

Finally they decided to use his religion as a plot against him. They knew he opened his window and prayed three times a day. They decided to have the king make a decree which would not allow prayer to anyone other than the king for a period of thirty days. The king was pleased, and the decree was issued. The decree, if not obeyed, would end in death. The person who disobeyed would be thrown into the lion's den.

The men who had encouraged the king to sign the decree were very happy. They hurried to the king to tell of Daniel's disobedience. They knew their plot had worked.

When the king was told about Daniel's prayers, he was very sorry, because he could not change the sealed law. There was nothing he could do to help save Daniel from the lion's den.

The king had Daniel brought in his court. He spoke sadly to him about his helplessness to save him. Then he said, "Your God, whom you serve so well, will deliver you."

The king's soldiers came and put Daniel into the lion's den. The king very sadly put his seal on the stone at the door of the den.

The king went home, but he was so miserable he was unable to eat or sleep.

The next day, the king got up very early and quickly hurried to the lion's den. As soon as he reached the den, he called out to Daniel.

Daniel replied to the king, "God has sent his angel to protect me, and he has shut the lion's mouths." King Darius was astonished to see Daniel alive and praising his God. Daniel's witness caused King Darius to call Daniel's God the true God, because no other god could do such marvelous things.

After King Darius died, King Cyrus came into power. Daniel continued to prosper under his rule.

What are some of the lessons we can learn from the choices made by Daniel? We need to learn early how to serve God and to choose to be obedient to his laws. We must always stand up for God, even when this loyalty means unpopular results—or even death. We must "dare to be a Daniel!" We must always be ready to witness for God to the unbelieving persons around us. Our lives should make them want to know our God. We must be faithful to pray daily and seek God's guidance.

Joseph

Joseph is often not given as much credit as he should be in the Christmas story. Joseph had to be an incredible man. He was chosen as an important part of God's plan for the birth of his Son.

Joseph was not only just, righteous, merciful, protective, and courageous, he was obedient to God. Joseph didn't hesitate to take Mary as his wife when the angel told him Mary was to bear the long-expected Messiah, Jesus. He obeyed. When the angel told him to flee to Egypt with Mary and Jesus, he was faithful to leave immediately. Joseph trusted God and faithfully did everything God asked him to do. God knew the heart of Joseph, and he entrusted Joseph with the unique job of providing a nurturing home life for his Son, Jesus.

We can see that God uses ordinary people to do his will on earth. Joseph was not a learned man. He was not a powerful man. He was not a wealthy man. He was a humble carpenter who was faithful to obey God's will in his life. We too must trust God—not ourselves—for our lives. We must be available if God chooses to use us.

Mary (Mother of Jesus)

In the sixth month, the angel Gabriel was sent from God to the city of Galilee, named Nazareth, to a virgin named Mary. Mary was espoused to a man named Joseph, who was from the house of David.

The angel came to her and said, "Hail thou that art highly favored, the Lord is with thee: blessed art thou among women."

When Mary saw the angel, she was troubled at his saying, and cast her mind what manner of salutation this should be.

The angel told her to fear not, because she had found favor with God. Gabriel told Mary she would conceive a child, and his name was to be called Jesus. The angel said, "He shall be great, and shall be called the Son of the Highest: and the Lord God shall give unto him the throne of his father David. He would reign over the house of Jacob, and of his kingdom there shall be no end."

Mary asked the angel how this could be, since she was a virgin. The angel answered, "The Holy Ghost shall come upon thee, and the power of the Highest shall overshadow thee: Therefore, that holy one which will be born of thee shall be called the Son of God." Mary then said, "Behold the handmaiden of the Lord; be it unto me according to thy holy word."

The song of praise Mary pours from her heart is found in Luke 1:46: "My soul doth magnify the Lord, and my spirit hath rejoiced in God my Savior. For he hath regarded the low estate of his handmaiden: for behold, from henceforth all generations shall call me blessed."

Mary was at first troubled when the angel Gabriel appeared to her. However, after she heard the voice of God speak to her heart, Mary chose to be a humble vessel of God. She showed obedience, selflessness, and virginal humility.

There are some important lessons to be learned from God's choice of Mary to bear his Son, Jesus. Mary was willing to trust God's plan for her life, even though she was engaged to marry Joseph. She humbly agreed to let God use her as a vessel to serve him. We, like Mary, must make the choice to be obedient to God's plan for our lives, even if it is not the plan we had chosen.

God's timing is not always our timing. At any point in our lives, we must be willing to believe like Mary. Nothing is impossible with God.

King Solomon

In 1 Kings 3:5–14, the Bible gives the account of Solomon becoming King of Israel at a young age. In Gibeon, the Lord appeared to Solomon in a dream by night, and God said, "Ask what I shall give thee."

Solomon wisely asked for understanding to discern the best for his people. The Lord was pleased, because Solomon did not ask for long life, riches, or the life of his enemies.

The Lord gave him a wise and understanding heart so that there was none before him or after him who would be like him. In addition to Solomon's request, God gave him riches and honor. God also promised to lengthen his days if he was obedient to God's commandments.

What can we learn from Solomon's wise choice? We need to be humble like Solomon. We need to realize it's not all about us. God wants us to honor and glorify Him in all we are entrusted by Him to complete. When we please God with our choices, our lives are enriched by his blessings. Psalm 37:4 says, "Delight thyself also in the Lord; and he shall give thee the desires of thine heart."

When Solomon became older, he made unwise choices in marrying heathen wives whose allegiance was not to God. These wives caused Solomon's heart to turn to other gods. The results of his sins caused God to become angry. God warned Solomon twice not to be involved with the idol worship of those wives. Solomon continued his disobedience. As a result of Solomon's disobedience, the kingdom of Israel was eventually divided and defeated. Only one tribe remained because of David.

What can we learn from Solomon's unwise choices? First of all, do not be unequally yoked to an unbelieving spouse. Secondly, unwise choices bring punishment from God.

Even wise people must be on guard, because they can choose unwisely if they fail to listen to the Holy Spirit.

Moses

Moses had two great works to do in his life. One was to bring the children of Israel out of the land of Egypt. The other important task was to write the first five books of the Bible. It was important that God's Word and laws be written for God's people.

In the life of Moses, God's plan for the protection of his life began very early.

The children of Israel were in captivity in Egypt. They were slaves, and they were ordered to do heavy labor. Even with the brutal labor, the children of Israel were multiplying faster than the Egyptians. The harsh Pharaoh became afraid they would be able to overtake the Egyptians' power and rule over them. The Pharaoh's fear caused him to issue an order which required all Israelite mothers to throw any newborn son into the river. They could keep the newborn girls. The little girls would not become soldiers who would be able to fight against the Egyptians.

Now during this time, a beautiful baby boy was born to a father and mother among the Israelites. The mother did not obey the order of Pharaoh. She hid her precious little boy for three months—but when he cried too loud, she knew he would be discovered.

Moses's mother chose to cover a wicker basket with tar and pitch. The child was placed into the basket, and the mother hid him in the reeds of the Nile. The child's sister was nearby so she could see what happened to her brother.

Pharaoh's daughter came down to bathe. While bathing, she spotted the basket and asked her maids to bring the basket to her. When the basket was opened, they saw the child crying. Pharaoh's daughter had compassion for the child, even though she recognized the child to be a Hebrew boy.

The child's sister saw what was happening. She came to Pharaoh's daughter and asked if see could find a nurse from the Hebrew women. Pharaoh's daughter said, "Go ahead." Of course, the sister gave the child to his own mother.

When Moses grew, his mother brought him to Pharaoh's daughter. The child became her own son. She named her son Moses, because she drew him out of the water.

Moses grew up in the king's palace and became a man. One day, he went out to the place where the Israelites were working. He saw an Egyptian cruelly beating a Hebrew slave. He became very angry at the horrible treatment of the slave. He carefully looked around, saw no one in sight, and killed the Egyptian. He buried the body in the sand.

The next day, two Hebrew slaves were fighting. Moses asked the offender why he was fighting his companion. The offending slave asked, "Who made you a judge over us? Are you intending to kill me, as you killed the Egyptian?"

Moses knew the incident would not be hidden and he would be in danger. He did not want to encounter the anger of Pharaoh. Pharaoh might have him killed.

Moses fled to Midian. Moses helped the priest of Midian's daughters water their flocks. He ended up living in their home. He eventually married Zipporah, the priest's daughter. They had a child named Gershom.

While Moses was living in Midian, the Egyptian Pharaoh died. The Hebrew people remained in bondage under the new Pharaoh. They began to cry to God to remember the covenant he made with Abraham, Isaac, and Jacob. God heard their cries and took notice of them.

One day, while Moses was shepherding the flock of Jethro, his father-in-law, he led the flock to Horeb, the mountain of God. While at Mount Horeb, God appeared to him in a burning bush. The bush kept burning, but was not consumed. Moses came near the bush to find out how the bush could keep on burning without being destroyed.

When the Lord saw he had Moses's attention, he called to him from the burning bush. The Lord said, "Moses, Moses!" Moses answered, "Here I am."

The Lord told Moses to take off his sandals, because he was on holy ground. God identified Himself to be the God of Abraham, Isaac, and Jacob. Moses hid his face, because he was afraid to look at God.

God told Moses he had heard the cry of his people in Egypt, and he planned to deliver them from the afflictions of the Egyptians. Then he told Moses he planned to use him to fulfill his plan of deliverance.

Moses stepped back. It had been forty years since he had left Egypt, and surely Pharaoh would have forgotten about his killing of the Egyptian, but he was afraid to go back.

Moses began to question God. Moses said to God, "Who am I that I should go to Pharaoh and bring the sons of Israel out of Egypt?"

God promised Moses, "Certainly I will be with you."

Moses knew the children of Israel had almost forgotten they had a God of their own, so Moses asked, "When I come to the children of Israel and say to them, 'The God of your fathers has sent me to you,' they will ask, 'Which God are you talking about?' What shall I say to them?"

God said to Moses, "Tell the children of Israel, I AM has sent me to you, the God of your fathers, the God of Abraham, the God of Isaac, and the God of Jacob: this is my name forever."

God told Moses to gather the elders of Israel and tell them he had heard the cries of his people in Egypt, and he planned to lead them out of Egypt into the land he had promised Abraham.

Moses again questioned God. "What if they don't believe me? They may say, 'God has not appeared to you.'"

God showed Moses three miracles God would use to empower him to convince the elders and the people to believe God had chosen Moses to deliver his people.

The first sign was the staff he was holding, which could be turned into a snake. The second sign was that his hand could be cured of leprosy. The third sign given Moses was his ability to turn water from the river into blood. Even after God let him do these miracles, Moses was not convinced he could accomplish the task God wanted him to do.

Moses began to offer an excuse. Moses said, "I am slow of speech and of a slow tongue." He did not want to go! He asked God to send someone else.

God wanted Moses to go. God said, "I know your brother Aaron can speak. You must tell him what I have said. Let him do the speaking to the people." Aaron would do the talking, and God would reveal the plans for deliverance to Moses.

God revealed to Moses the hard heart of Pharaoh. Moses used the miracle of the rod and the miracle of turning the river to blood, and still Pharaoh's heart was hard. He would not let the people go. Then the plagues begin to cover all Egypt—the plagues of frogs, lice, flies, a dreadful sickness which killed the animals, hail, locusts, a great darkness over all Egypt, and the death of the firstborn in every Egyptian home.

The power of God to bring these plagues on the Egyptians and to exclude the Israelites showed the people that God had not forgotten his promise to their fathers. The Egyptians saw the power of the one true God of the Hebrews and knew this God was not like their heathen gods. God had let Pharaoh's heart be hardened so the people could see his power and worship him.

Finally, Pharaoh agreed to let God's people go. Moses was able to lead the people into the wilderness. God provided the food and water they needed. However, many times they were "stiff-necked" and disobeyed God's commandments. They grumbled and complained to Moses for every problem.

Moses became angry with the people for not trusting God. It was hard to believe the people did not trust God after all the miracles, love, and protection he had provided for them.

At one particular time, the people were grumbling about not having water to drink in the Desert of Zin. The whole congregation gathered against Moses and Aaron. They begin to question why they were brought in the wilderness to die. They complained there was no seed, figs, pomegranates, or water to drink.

Moses and Aaron left the assembly of the congregation and went to inquire of God at the door of the tabernacle of the congregation.

God spoke to Moses. He told Moses and Aaron to gather the assembly together and to speak to the rock before their eyes and it would give forth God's water. The water would be enough for the people and their beasts.

Moses and Aaron called the congregation before the rock and said to them, "Hear now, ye rebels; must we fetch you water out of this rock?" Moses then lifted his hand with his rod and struck it twice. Water came out abundantly, and the congregation and their beasts drank.

Then God spoke to Moses and Aaron. God said, "Because ye believed me not, to sanctify me in the eyes of the children of Israel, therefore ye shall not bring this congregation into the land which I have given them."

What are some of the lessons we can learn from the life of Moses? God uses ordinary men and women to do extraordinary tasks. When God chooses a person to do his will here on earth, he qualifies them, and he will guide and protect them. We can see how Moses failed to give God the credit and honor he deserved when the people complained in the Desert of Zin. Because he failed to honor God before his people, Moses missed the blessing of entering the Promised Land. We must realize when we do not choose to give God his honor and glory, we will miss the blessing just like Moses.

Rahab

The life of Rahab is found in the book of Joshua. After the death of Moses, Joshua was chosen by God to lead the children of Israel into the land promised to them.

Joshua sent two men to spy, secretly saying, "Go view the land, even Jericho." The two men went into the land. They lodged at the house of Rahab, the harlot.

The king of Jericho heard about the spies who were searching his country. The king sent a message to Rahab, telling her the men she had in her house were spies, and she was ordered to bring forth the men.

Rahab took the two men and hid them. When the men came to search her house, she told them two men did indeed come to her house, but she did not know they were spies. Rahab told the king's men the two men left at dark—about the time the gate was closed. She said she did not know where they had planned to go, but if they would hurry, they might be able to overtake the spies.

After the king's men left to hunt the spies, Rahab went to the roof of her house. She had hidden the men with stalks of flax on her roof.

Before the men had time to sleep, Rahab had a talk with them. She revealed her heart to them. She told them their God had revealed to her all about their purpose for being in their country. She admitted she knew their God had given the children of Israel her country. Rahab admitted that all the inhabitants of her country were terrified of the power of this God. Her people had heard about their God drying up the Red Sea so his people could escape from the Egyptians. They heard about the many Egyptians who tried to cross the water behind God's people and drowned when the water of the sea quickly covered them. They also had heard about the defeat of the two Amorite kings.

Rahab made a profound statement when she admitted her own fear and the fear of her country because of their God. The statement she made was: "The Lord your God, he is God in heaven above, and in the earth beneath."

After she made her profession of faith in their God, she asked for protection for herself and her father's household. The men listened to Rehab's story and her profession of faith.

The men promised to give her and her father's household the protection she had asked of them it she promised not to utter their business to anyone. She agreed to keep their secret.

Rahab helped them escape from her house. She used a cord from her window to let them down. Her house was located on the town wall.

Rahab advised them to hide in the mountains for three days. After that time, their pursuers would have returned from looking for them.

The men promised with an oath to save her and her father's household. The men told Rahab to bring her father's household into her house so they would be safe.

A scarlet thread was to be placed in the same window they escaped. The thread was to be a sign of their oath and its protection.

The spies returned to Joshua. The news was good. They had learned of the people's fear of their God. They were confident their God had already delivered the land into their hands.

The fall of Jericho was completed. The city was accursed, and all within it perished. Only Rahab and those safe in her house were spared, because she made the choice to hide the messengers sent to spy on Jericho.

What can we learn from Rehab's choice?

1. God uses the most unlikely people to carry out his will on earth! Rahab was a harlot!

2. God changes the hearts of ungodly people's lives, and he uses them in mysterious and marvelous ways.

3. The witness of believers can impact others to believe and desire to serve God.

4. In some cases, a choice can literally mean life or death. Rahab saved her life by making a right choice to change the direction of her life. Rahab went from being a pagan harlot to being a believer of God and his sovereign power over heaven and earth.

5. God was not through with Rahab; she is named in the genealogy of Christ.

6. God's grace is sufficient to cover all sins!

Saul/Paul

In the book of Acts, we first read about Saul of Tarsus, a persecutor of the Christians. Saul was a "Hebrew of the Hebrews," a Pharisee, and a member of the tribe of Benjamin.

Saul's parents lived in the heathen city of Tarsus. They did not want their son to grow up not knowing God. Saul was sent to the finest school in Jerusalem. He studied under the wise doctor of law, Gamaliel. Rabbi Gamaliel was a leading authority in the Sanhedrin. Gamaliel had advised the Pharisees to leave the Christians alone.

Saul had studied the Old Testament well. He was strict in keeping the laws and in doing what he thought was right. Saul believed the followers of Jesus were teaching wrong things and that they were against God. He felt it was his duty to stop the teachings of Jesus. Because of Saul, many Christians were put in prison or killed. Saul held the coats of the men who killed Stephen.

Saul went to the high priest and told them the new religion had to be stamped out. Saul asked the high priest to give him letters to the priest in Damascus giving him permission to arrest the followers of Jesus.

Saul set out with a few men to travel to Damascus. After traveling a few days and nights, they were near the city. Suddenly, a light streamed from heaven, brighter than the light of the sun. The men were so startled and blinded by the bright light that they all fell to the ground.

Saul heard a voice from heaven saying, "Saul, Saul, why do you persecute me?" Saul was very frightened. He trembled with fear. He asked, "Who is speaking to me?"

The voice said, "I am Jesus of Nazareth. I am the one you are persecuting."

Saul was surprised. He thought he was right, and the followers of Jesus were wrong. He thought God was pleased with him. When he heard the voice of Jesus, he realized he was wrong, and he was actually fighting against God.

Saul cried out, "Lord, what do you want me to do?"

Jesus answered, "Stand up, Saul. I have appeared to you to show you that after this, you are not to fight against me any more. You are to become one of my disciples, and you will tell everybody about me. I will appear to you again and show you more about myself. Go to Damascus, and there it shall be told to you what you must do."

After meeting Jesus on the road to Damascus, Saul's direction in life was forever changed. The glory of God's light blinded Saul for three days.

When Saul finally arrived at the house of Judas, he sat in his house without eating and drinking. He wanted to think about what had happened to him.

Saul thought about the fine education he had experienced under the great teacher, Gamaliel. He thought about the Old Testament and the things it said about Jesus. He had time to review all the Old Testament prophecies and how Jesus had fulfilled these prophecies.

The rest is history—Saul's name was changed to Paul. The Gospel of Jesus was given to the entire world by Paul's faithful obedience to the call of Jesus on the road to Damascus.

What are some of the lessons we can learn from the life of Paul?

1. God can change the heart of the most evil sinner and use them to accomplish his work on earth.
2. When we believe Jesus is the Son of God, and we accept his power, grace, and salvation in our lives, then we will be like Paul and will share this hope with the world around us. We will be his witnesses.

Criminals on the Cross

The conversations between Jesus and the two criminals can be found in Luke 23. Jesus was crucified with a criminal on each side of Him.

There were three crosses at Calvary. Jesus was crucified between the two men. All three were led to the crosses. As they walked together, they saw Jesus endure the mocking crowds without a word. They heard the crowds deriding Jesus, saying, "He saved others, let him save Himself." Both criminals heard Him pray, "Father, forgive them; for they know not what they do."

One of the criminals hanging beside Jesus on the cross said, "Are you not the Christ? Save yourself and us!" The other criminal rebuked him, saying, "Do you not even fear God, since you are under the same sentence of condemnation? And we indeed justly, we are receiving what we deserve for our deeds; but this man has done nothing wrong." Then he said, "Jesus, remember me when you come in your kingdom."

Jesus said to the criminal, "Truly I say to you, today you shall be with me in Paradise."

What are some important lessons we can learn from the choices of the two criminals?

1. Jesus is always ready to forgive a repentant sinner. Even a deathbed conversion is accepted.
2. Salvation is through Jesus alone. Good works does not earn a person the right to paradise. The criminal had no chance for good works. Sadly, those who make deathbed decisions to accept Jesus miss the blessings of their life on earth.
3. The criminals' choices determined their eternal destinies. Both criminals had the same ability to choose to follow Jesus or continue to be loyal to Satan. As a result of the right choice, the one repentant criminal gained forgiveness and Paradise. The other sadly made the choice to live in hell's torment eternally and live in separation from God.
4. After death, we all must meet our Creator God.

King David

David was a key person in the Old Testament. He wrote the often quoted and the beautiful book of Psalms.

1 Samuel and 2 Samuel tell the story of King Saul's sin of rejection and disobedience to the Word of the Lord. As a result of Saul's sins, the Lord chose David to replace Saul as King of Israel.

God sent Samuel, the prophet, to the household of Jesse. Jesse had several sons, and Samuel was to choose the one God wanted as a replacement for King Saul. All of Jesse's sons were brought before Samuel. The youngest son, David, was the last one to appear before Samuel. The Lord told Samuel that David was to be anointed as the next king of Israel.

God choose David, because God looks at the heart rather than the appearance of a person. God said, "I have found David, the son of Jesse, a man after My heart, who will do all my will. From the offspring of this man according to promise God has brought to Israel a Savior, Jesus" (Acts 13:22).

David was a mighty warrior, and the Spirit of the Lord was upon him. David killed the giant, Goliath, with a slingshot. The Philistines feared David.

David's fame as a mighty warrior caused King Saul to become jealous of his accomplishments. Saul sought to kill David. David had to flee from Saul's anger and his plot to kill him.

King Saul was killed in a battle with the Philistines. After his death, David was anointed king over Israel.

David continued to be a powerful warrior. His troops destroyed the children of Ammon and besieged Rabbath. After his great victory, David tarried in Jerusalem.

In the evening, David walked on his roof. He saw a beautiful woman washing herself. David inquired about her. He learned she was called Bathsheba, and she was married to Uriah, the Hittite.

David was so smitten with Bathsheba, he sent messengers to bring her to him. David's desire caused him to commit adultery with Bathsheba, who was married.

After Bathsheba returned home, she discovered she was with child. She knew the child was not her husband's, because he had been in battle. He had been absent from seeing his wife for a while. Bathsheba sent a message to King David to tell him she was with child.

When David heard Bathsheba was carrying his child, he began to plot a way to cover his sin. He called Uriah from the battle and inquired about the progress of the battle. Then he gave Uriah permission to go home to his wife and rest from the battle.

Uriah told King David he did not want to go home for a rest. Uriah did not want to desert his fellow warriors. David soon realized this man could not be used to cover his sin.

When David realized Uriah would not go home to his wife, he had to devise another scheme to protect himself and Bathsheba. David's plan becomes even more evil. He decided he would have Uriah sent to the front of the battle. This evil plan would cause the death of Uriah.

Uriah was killed, and Bathsheba was notified her husband had died in battle. As was the custom of her people, Bathsheba mourned for her husband.

After the period of mourning was over, King David sent for Bathsheba. She became his wife, and they had a son.

Nathan, God's prophet, was sent to the king to tell him God was displeased with his sins of adultery and murder. When confronted with his sins, David was very sorry, and he begged God to forgive him. God did forgive him, but David had to suffer the consequences of a wrong choice.

David and Bathsheba had to suffer the horrible agony of seeing their child become very sick. Even after much prayer and begging God for their child's life, God allowed the child to die. In addition to the death of the child, God told David the sword would never depart from his house.

What lessons can we learn from David's choice?

1. Temptation can overtake even the most godly men and women.
2. We must be on the alert for Satan's schemes and ask God to help us resolve to make the right choice and obey Him.
3. There is forgiveness for our sins, no matter how evil.
4. We must remember that there is a price to pay for sin. The price we pay is the unwanted circumstances which remain even after we have been forgiven.

Conclusion

I hope wisdom has been gained by reading this book. These collections of wisdom are written to give all who read this book the desire to make wiser choices. I hope the older generation who reads this book will share this wisdom with the younger generations to follow.

Some people who read this book have—by the grace of God—made wise choices. Their lives have had only a few bad consequences from poor decisions. Hopefully for these readers, this book will reinforce and encourage them to continue making the right choices.

There will be some people who read this book who will say, "It is too late for me, and I'm not worthy of God's love. All or most of my major decisions have been wrong choices. These choices are causing me to suffer terrible consequences."

A person suffering because of poor choices can choose to make wise choices. God has given all who desire to change the direction of their life a second chance.

The important thing to remember is that it is never too late to change life's direction. God is always ready to accept a sincere desire to obey and serve him.

Another important thing to remember is that Jesus takes a person just as they are. A person does not have to wait until they are good enough. None of us can ever be worthy. A person must be willing to give themselves to God just as they are, with all their fighting, fears, hate, love, pride, and the shame of their past sins.

When a person is willing to give their heart to Jesus just as they are, Jesus will welcome and pardon them with his love and grace. In order to receive God's gift of salvation, a person must *believe.* John, an apostle of Christ, says in John 3:16, "For God so loved the world that he gave his only begotten son, that whosoever believes in him shall nor perish, but have eternal life." A person must accept the gift of God's love and believe in his grace to forgive their sins and give them life eternal.

The second step in God's plan of salvation is to *confess* all sins and to be humble before God. 1 John 1:9 says, "If we confess our sins, he is faithful and just to forgive us our sins, and to cleanse us from all our unrighteousness."

After a person confesses their sins, *humility* must follow. The person must acknowledge that they can do nothing without God's grace. Paul writes in Ephesians 2:8, "For by grace you have been saved through faith; and that not of yourselves, it is the gift of God; not a result of works, that no one should boast."

The third requirement for Salvation is to *repent.* To repent means a person is truly sorry for their sins and they choose to change from their sinful ways.

Once a person has *believed, confessed,* and *repented,* they are one of God's redeemed. They are God's forever. When a person becomes a believer, they can claim God's promises in the following bible verses:

"In whom you also trusted, after that ye heard the word of truth, the gospel of your salvation: in whom also after that ye believed, ye were sealed with that Holy Spirit of promise" (Ephesians 1:13).

"For he has said, I will never leave thee, nor forsake thee" (Hebrews 13:5).

"For I am persuaded that neither death, nor life, nor angels, nor principalities, nor powers, nor things present, nor things to come, nor height, nor depth, nor any other creature, shall be able to separate us from the love of God, which is in Christ Jesus our Lord" (Romans 8:38–39).

When a person experiences the grace and forgiveness of Jesus' salvation, they will want to share it with others, and they will want to tell others that God will give them the same forgiveness and love. If a person believes and desires to serve God, they become a new person in Christ.

Mother Teresa, a nun who worked in the slums, rightly said, "You will never know that Christ is all you need until Christ is all you have."

Works Cited

Some of the books and articles which influenced my thoughts were found in the following books:

Unless otherwise identified, Scripture quotations are from the authorized version of The King James Bible.

The New American Standard Bible

The Anderson Independent, May 9, 1970.

Allen, Charles. *God's Psychiatry*. Revell. 1970.

Blanchard, John. *Gathered Gold: A Treasury of Quotations for Christians*. Darlington, Co.: Evangelical Press. 1989.

Elliot, Elizabeth. *Passion and Purity*. Grand Rapids: Revell.1993.

Elwell, Ellen Banks. *The Christian Mom's Idea Book*. Wheaton: Crossway. 1997.

Graham, Billy. "In My Opinion." *The Charlotte Observer*. July 28, 2007.

Kinkade, Thomas. *Garden of Friendship*. Nashville: Thomas Nelson. 1982.

Maxwell, John. "Six Things Children Need." *Decision Magazine*, March 1998.

Petty, Jo. *Wings of Silver*. Norwalk: Gibson, 1967.

<u>*Presbyterian Journal,*</u> September 8, 1982.

Rabon, Christine, Collection of Notes Unpublished, 1940-1989

Tripp, Tedd. *Shepherding a Child's Heart.* Wapwallopin: SP Press. 1995.

A 20 Day Study in Stewardship C. 1997 Redeemer Presbyterian Church New York

White, Joe. Twenty ways to tell your child "I love you." *Focus on the Family.* May 1996.

About the Author

Carolyn Gault, lives with her husband, Horace "Buddy" F. Gault Jr., in Rock Hill, South Carolina. They have been married for forty-six years. They have two grown daughters and four grandchildren.

Carolyn is a graduate of the University of South Carolina. She received a Bachelor of Arts degree in Sociology and a minor in Psychology.

After graduation, she worked for several years as a caseworker for the Social Services Department in Spartanburg, SC.

Carolyn married Buddy, and his job moved them to Rock Hill. In Rock Hill, she was busy raising their two daughters. She also helped in their family-owned drug stores. She was their secretary and treasurer of their business.

Carolyn has been reading her Bible daily since her pre-teen years. She has been blessed to have studied under some of the best Bible teachers and pastors and has participated in excellent Bible seminars.

Over the years, Carolyn has taught Sunday school, lead youth groups, held Friendship Bible studies in her home, and taught Bible classes for ladies at her church.

She does not claim to be an authority on the topics covered in this book. However, she has used many of the ideas and much of the wisdom given in this book as a guideline for her own life choices.

Carolyn hopes sharing the ideas and wisdom she has gained from her own life experiences will help the younger generation to make wiser choices.